THE PENGUIN POETS

SELECTED POEMS

John Ashbery is the author of fifteen books of poetry, including *April Galleons*, *Flow Chart*, and *Hotel Lautréamont*, and a volume of art criticism, *Reported Sightings*. His *Self-Portrait in a Convex Mirror* received the Pulitzer Prize for poetry, as well as the National Book Critics Circle Award and the National Book Award. He has been named a Guggenheim Fellow and a MacArthur Fellow, and is a chancellor of the Academy of American Poets. In 1989–1990 he was Charles Eliot Norton Professor of Poetry at Harvard. He is currently Charles P. Stevenson, Jr., Professor of Literature at Bard College.

Also by John Ashbery

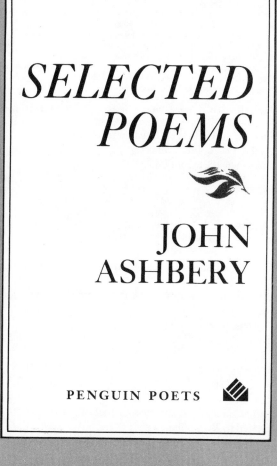

SELECTED POEMS

JOHN ASHBERY

PENGUIN POETS

PENGUIN BOOKS
Published by the Penguin Group
Penguin Group (USA) Inc., 375 Hudson Street, New Y rk, New York 10014, U.S.A.
Penguin Group (Canada), 90 Eglinton Avenue East, Suite 700, T ronto,
   Ontario, Canada M4P 2Y3 (a division of Pearson Penguin Canada Inc.)
Penguin Books Ltd, 80 Strand, London WC2R 0RL, England
Penguin Ireland, 25 St Stephen's Green, Dublin 2, Ireland (a division of Penguin Books Ltd)
Penguin Group (Australia), 250 Camberwell Road, Camberwell,
   ictoria 3124, Australia (a division of Pearson Australia Group Pty Ltd)
Penguin Books India Pvt Ltd, 11 Community Centre, Panchsheel Park, New Delhi – 110 017, India
Penguin Group (NZ), cnr Airborne and Rosedale Roads,
   Albany, Auckland 1310, New Zealand (a division of Pearson New Zealand Ltd)
Penguin Books (South Africa) (Pty) Ltd, 24 Sturdee A
   Rosebank, Johannesburg 2196, South Africa

Penguin Books Ltd, Registered Offices: 80 Strand, London WC2R 0RL, England

First published in the United States of America by
Viking Penguin Inc. 1985
Published in Penguin Books 1986

20

Page 349 constitutes an extension of this copyright page.

LIBRARY OF CONGRESS CATALOGING IN PUBLICATION DATA
Ashbery, John.
Selected poems.
Includes index.
I. Title.
[PS3501.S475A6   1986]   811'.54   86-9521
ISBN 0 14 058.553 2

Printed in the United States of America
Design by Beth Tondreau
Set in Janson

CONTENTS

From *SOME TREES*

From *THE TENNIS COURT OATH*

From *RIVERS AND MOUNTAINS*

From *THE DOUBLE DREAM OF SPRING*

From *THREE POEMS*

From *SELF-PORTRAIT IN A CONVEX MIRROR*

From *A WAVE*

From
SOME
TREES

TWO SCENES

I

We see us as we truly behave:
From every corner comes a distinctive offering.
The train comes bearing joy;
The sparks it strikes illuminate the table.
Destiny guides the water-pilot, and it is destiny.
For long we hadn't heard so much news, such noise.
The day was warm and pleasant.
"We see you in your hair,
Air resting around the tips of mountains."

II

A fine rain anoints the canal machinery.
This is perhaps a day of general honesty
Without example in the world's history
Though the fumes are not of a singular authority
And indeed are dry as poverty.
Terrific units are on an old man
In the blue shadow of some paint cans
As laughing cadets say, "In the evening
Everything has a schedule, if you can find out what it is."

POPULAR SONGS

He continued to consult her for her beauty
(The host gone to a longing grave).
The story then resumed in day coaches
Both bravely eyed the finer dust on the blue. That summer
("The worst ever") she stayed in the car with the cur.
That was something between her legs.
Alton had been getting letters from his mother
About the payments—half the flood
Over and what about the net rest of the year?
Who cares? Anyway (you know how thirsty they were)
The extra worry began it—on the
Blue blue mountain—she never set foot
And then and there. Meanwhile the host
Mourned her quiet tenure. They all stayed chatting.
No one did much about eating.
The tears came and stopped, came and stopped, until
Becoming the guano-lightened summer night landscape,
All one glow, one mild laugh lasting ages.
Some precision, he fumed into his soup.

You laugh. There is no peace in the fountain.
The footmen smile and shift. The mountain
Rises nightly to disappointed stands
Dining in "The Gardens of the Moon."
There is no way to prevent this
Or the expectation of disappointment.
All are aware, some carry a secret
Better, of hands emulating deeds
Of days untrustworthy. But these may decide.
The face extended its sorrowing light
Far out over them. And now silent as a group
The actors prepare their first decline.

THE INSTRUCTION MANUAL

As I sit looking out of a window of the building
I wish I did not have to write the instruction manual on the uses
  of a new metal.
I look down into the street and see people, each walking with an
  inner peace,
And envy them—they are so far away from me!
Not one of them has to worry about getting out this manual on
  schedule.
And, as my way is, I begin to dream, resting my elbows on the desk
  and leaning out of the window a little,
Of dim Guadalajara! City of rose-colored flowers!
City I wanted most to see, and most did not see, in Mexico!
But I fancy I see, under the press of having to write the instruction
  manual,
Your public square, city, with its elaborate little bandstand!
The band is playing *Scheherazade* by Rimsky-Korsakov.
Around stand the flower girls, handing out rose- and lemon-colored
  flowers,
Each attractive in her rose-and-blue striped dress (Oh! such shades of
  rose and blue),
And nearby is the little white booth where women in green serve you
  green and yellow fruit.
The couples are parading; everyone is in a holiday mood.
First, leading the parade, is a dapper fellow
Clothed in deep blue. On his head sits a white hat
And he wears a mustache, which has been trimmed for the occasion.
His dear one, his wife, is young and pretty; her shawl is rose, pink, and
  white.
Her slippers are patent leather, in the American fashion,
And she carries a fan, for she is modest, and does not want the crowd
  to see her face too often.
But everybody is so busy with his wife or loved one

I doubt they would notice the mustachioed man's wife.
Here come the boys! They are skipping and throwing little things on
  the sidewalk
Which is made of gray tile. One of them, a little older, has a toothpick
  in his teeth.
He is silenter than the rest, and affects not to notice the pretty young
  girls in white.
But his friends notice them, and shout their jeers at the laughing girls.
Yet soon all this will cease, with the deepening of their years,
And love bring each to the parade grounds for another reason.
But I have lost sight of the young fellow with the toothpick.
Wait—there he is—on the other side of the bandstand,
Secluded from his friends, in earnest talk with a young girl
Of fourteen or fifteen. I try to hear what they are saying
But it seems they are just mumbling something—shy words of
  love, probably.
She is slightly taller than he, and looks quietly down into his
  sincere eyes.
She is wearing white. The breeze ruffles her long fine black hair
  against her olive cheek.
Obviously she is in love. The boy, the young boy with the toothpick,
  he is in love too;
His eyes show it. Turning from this couple,
I see there is an intermission in the concert.
The paraders are resting and sipping drinks through straws
(The drinks are dispensed from a large glass crock by a lady in
  dark blue),
And the musicians mingle among them, in their creamy white
  uniforms, and talk
About the weather, perhaps, or how their kids are doing at school.

Let us take this opportunity to tiptoe into one of the side streets.
Here you may see one of those white houses with green trim

That are so popular here. Look—I told you!

It is cool and dim inside, but the patio is sunny.

An old woman in gray sits there, fanning herself with a palm leaf fan.

She welcomes us to her patio, and offers us a cooling drink.

"My son is in Mexico City," she says. "He would welcome you too

If he were here. But his job is with a bank there.

Look, here is a photograph of him."

And a dark-skinned lad with pearly teeth grins out at us from the worn
  leather frame.

We thank her for her hospitality, for it is getting late

And we must catch a view of the city, before we leave, from a good
  high place.

That church tower will do—the faded pink one, there against the fierce
  blue of the sky. Slowly we enter.

The caretaker, an old man dressed in brown and gray, asks us how long
  we have been in the city, and how we like it here.

His daughter is scrubbing the steps—she nods to us as we pass into the
  tower.

Soon we have reached the top, and the whole network of the city
  extends before us.

There is the rich quarter, with its houses of pink and white, and its
  crumbling, leafy terraces.

There is the poorer quarter, its homes a deep blue.

There is the market, where men are selling hats and swatting flies

And there is the public library, painted several shades of pale green and
  beige.

Look! There is the square we just came from, with the promenaders.

There are fewer of them, now that the heat of the day has increased,

But the young boy and girl still lurk in the shadows of the
  bandstand.

And there is the home of the little old lady—

She is still sitting in the patio, fanning herself.

How limited, but how complete withal, has been our experience of
  Guadalajara!

We have seen young love, married love, and the love of an aged mother
  for her son.
We have heard the music, tasted the drinks, and looked at colored
  houses.
What more is there to do, except stay? And that we cannot do.
And as a last breeze freshens the top of the weathered old tower, I turn
  my gaze
Back to the instruction manual which has made me dream of
  Guadalajara.

THE GRAPEVINE

Of who we and all they are
You all now know. But you know
After they began to find us out we grew
Before they died thinking us the causes

Of their acts. Now we'll not know
The truth of some still at the piano, though
They often date from us, causing
These changes we think we are. We don't care

Though, so tall up there
In young air. But things get darker as we move
To ask them: Whom must we get to know
To die, so you live and we know?

A BOY

I'll do what the raids suggest,
Dad, and that other livid window,
But the tide pushes an awful lot of monsters
And I think it's my true fate.

*It had been raining but
It had not been raining.*

No one could begin to mop up this particular mess.
Thunder lay down in the heart.
"My child, I love any vast electrical disturbance."
Disturbance! Could the old man, face in the rainweed,

Ask more smuttily? By night it charged over plains,
Driven from Dallas and Oregon, always *whither*,
Why not now? The boy seemed to have fallen
From shelf to shelf of someone's rage.

That night it rained on the boxcars, explaining
The thought of the pensive cabbage roses near the boxcars.
My boy. Isn't there something I asked you once?
What happened? It's also farther to the corner
Aboard the maple furniture. *He
Couldn't lie.* He'd tell 'em by their syntax.

But listen now in the flood.
They're throwing up behind the lines.
Dry fields of lightning rise to receive
The observer, the mincing flag. *An unendurable age.*

GLAZUNOVIANA

The man with the red hat
And the polar bear, is he here too?
The window giving on shade,
Is that here too?
And all the little helps,
My initials in the sky,
The hay of an arctic summer night?

The bear
Drops dead in sight of the window.
Lovely tribes have just moved to the north.
In the flickering evening the martins grow denser.
Rivers of wings surround us and vast tribulation.

THE PICTURE OF LITTLE J. A.
IN A PROSPECT OF FLOWERS

He was spoilt from childhood
by the future, which he mastered
rather early and apparently
without great difficulty.
      BORIS PASTERNAK

I
Darkness falls like a wet sponge
And Dick gives Genevieve a swift punch
In the pajamas. "Aroint thee, witch."
Her tongue from previous ecstasy
Releases thoughts like little hats.

"He clap'd me first during the eclipse.
Afterwards I noted his manner
Much altered. But he sending
At that time certain handsome jewels
I durst not seem to take offence."

In a far recess of summer
Monks are playing soccer.

II
So far is goodness a mere memory
Or naming of recent scenes of badness
That even these lives, children,
You may pass through to be blessed,
So fair does each invent his virtue.

And coming from a white world, music
Will sparkle at the lips of many who are

Beloved. Then these, as dirty handmaidens
To some transparent witch, will dream
Of a white hero's subtle wooing,
And time shall force a gift on each.

That beggar to whom you gave no cent
Striped the night with his strange descant.

III
Yet I cannot escape the picture
Of my small self in that bank of flowers:
My head among the blazing phlox
Seemed a pale and gigantic fungus.
I had a hard stare, accepting

Everything, taking nothing,
As though the rolled-up future might stink
As loud as stood the sick moment
The shutter clicked. Though I was wrong,
Still, as the loveliest feelings

Must soon find words, and these, yes,
Displace them, so I am not wrong
In calling this comic version of myself
The true one. For as change is horror,
Virtue is really stubbornness

And only in the light of lost words
Can we imagine our rewards.

SONNET

Each servant stamps the reader with a look.
After many years he has been brought nothing.
The servant's frown is the reader's patience.
The servant goes to bed.
The patience rambles on
Musing on the library's lofty holes.

His pain is the servant's alive.
It pushes to the top stain of the wall
Its tree-top's head of excitement:
Baskets, birds, beetles, spools.
The light walls collapse next day.
Traffic is the reader's pictured face.
Dear, be the tree your sleep awaits;
Worms be your words, you not safe from ours.

THE YOUNG SON

The screen of supreme good fortune curved his absolute smile into a celestial scream. These things (the most arbitrary that could exist) wakened denials, thoughts of putrid reversals as he traced the green paths to and fro. Here and there a bird sang, a rose silenced her expression of him, and all the gaga flowers wondered. But they puzzled the wanderer with their vague wearinesses. Is the conclusion, he asked, the road forced by concubines from exact meters of strategy? Surely the trees are hinged to no definite purpose or surface. Yet now a wonder would shoot up, all one hue, and virtues would jostle each other to get a view of nothing—the crowded house, two faces glued fast to the mirror, corners and the bustling forest ever preparing, ever menacing its own shape with a shadow of the evil defenses gotten up and in fact already exhausted in some void of darkness, some kingdom he knew the earth could not even bother to avoid if the minutes arranged and divine lettermen with smiling cries were to come in the evening of administration and night which no cure, no bird ever more compulsory, no subject apparently intent on its heart's own demon would forestall even if the truths she told of were now being seriously lit, one by one, in the hushed and fast darkening room.

ERRORS

Jealousy. Whispered weather reports.
In the street we found boxes
Littered with snow, to burn at home.
What flower tolling on the waters,
You stupefied me. We waxed,
Carnivores, late and alight
In the beaded winter. All was ominous, luminous.
Beyond the bed's veils the white walls danced
Some violent compunction. Promises,
We thought then of your dry portals,
Bright cornices of eavesdropping palaces,
You were painfully stitched to hours
The moon now tears up, scoffing at the unrinsed portions.
And loves adopted realm. Flees to water,
The coach dissolving in mists.
                              A wish
Refines the lines around the mouth
At these ten-year intervals. It fumed
Clear air of wars. It desired
Excess of core in all things. From all things sucked
A glossy denial. But look, pale day:
We fly hence. To return if sketched
In the prophet's silence. Who doubts it is true?

ILLUSTRATION

I
A novice was sitting on a cornice
High over the city. Angels

Combined their prayers with those
Of the police, begging her to come off it.

One lady promised to be her friend.
"I do not want a friend," she said.

A mother offered her some nylons
Stripped from her very legs. Others brought

Little offerings of fruit and candy,
The blind man all his flowers. If any

Could be called successful, these were,
For that the scene should be a ceremony

Was what she wanted. "I desire
Monuments," she said. "I want to move

Figuratively, as waves caress
The thoughtless shore. You people I know

Will offer me every good thing
I do not want. But please remember

I died accepting them." With that, the wind
Unpinned her bulky robes, and naked

As a roc's egg, she drifted softly downward
Out of the angels' tenderness and the minds of men.

II

Much that is beautiful must be discarded
So that we may resemble a taller

Impression of ourselves. Moths climb in the flame,
Alas, that wish only to be the flame:

They do not lessen our stature.
We twinkle under the weight

Of indiscretions. But how could we tell
That of the truth we know, she was

The somber vestment? For that night, rockets sighed
Elegantly over the city, and there was feasting:

There is so much in that moment!
So many attitudes toward that flame,

We might have soared from earth, watching her glide
Aloft, in her peplum of bright leaves.

But she, of course, was only an effigy
Of indifference, a miracle

Not meant for us, as the leaves are not
Winter's because it is the end.

SOME TREES

These are amazing: each
Joining a neighbor, as though speech
Were a still performance.
Arranging by chance

To meet as far this morning
From the world as agreeing
With it, you and I
Are suddenly what the trees try

To tell us we are:
That their merely being there
Means something; that soon
We may touch, love, explain.

And glad not to have invented
Such comeliness, we are surrounded:
A silence already filled with noises,
A canvas on which emerges

A chorus of smiles, a winter morning.
Placed in a puzzling light, and moving,
Our days put on such reticence
These accents seem their own defense.

THE PAINTER

Sitting between the sea and the buildings
He enjoyed painting the sea's portrait.
But just as children imagine a prayer
Is merely silence, he expected his subject
To rush up the sand, and, seizing a brush,
Plaster its own portrait on the canvas.

So there was never any paint on his canvas
Until the people who lived in the buildings
Put him to work: "Try using the brush
As a means to an end. Select, for a portrait,
Something less angry and large, and more subject
To a painter's moods, or, perhaps, to a prayer."

How could he explain to them his prayer
That nature, not art, might usurp the canvas?
He chose his wife for a new subject,
Making her vast, like ruined buildings,
As if, forgetting itself, the portrait
Had expressed itself without a brush.

Slightly encouraged, he dipped his brush
In the sea, murmuring a heartfelt prayer:
"My soul, when I paint this next portrait
Let it be you who wrecks the canvas."
The news spread like wildfire through the buildings:
He had gone back to the sea for his subject.

Imagine a painter crucified by his subject!
Too exhausted even to lift his brush,
He provoked some artists leaning from the buildings
To malicious mirth: "We haven't a prayer
Now, of putting ourselves on canvas,
Or getting the sea to sit for a portrait!"

Others declared it a self-portrait.
Finally all indications of a subject
Began to fade, leaving the canvas
Perfectly white. He put down the brush.
At once a howl, that was also a prayer,
Arose from the overcrowded buildings.

They tossed him, the portrait, from the tallest of the buildings;
And the sea devoured the canvas and the brush
As though his subject had decided to remain a prayer.

AND YOU KNOW

The girls, protected by gold wire from the gaze
Of the onrushing students, live in an atmosphere of vacuum
In the old schoolhouse covered with nasturtiums.
At night, comets, shootings stars, twirling planets,
Suns, bits of illuminated pumice, and spooks hang over the old place;
The atmosphere is breathless. Some find the summer light
Nauseous and damp, but there are those
Who are charmed by it, going out into the morning.
We must rest here, for this is where the teacher comes.
On his desk stands a vase of tears.
A quiet feeling pervades the playroom. His voice clears
Through the interminable afternoon: "I was a child once
Under the spangled sun. Now I do what must be done.
I teach reading and writing and flaming arithmetic. Those
In my home come to me anxiously at night, asking how it goes.
My door is always open. I never lie, and the great heat warms me."

His door is always open, the fond schoolmaster!
We ought to imitate him in our lives,
For as a man lives, he dies. To pass away
In the afternoon, on the vast vapid bank
You think is coming to crown you with hollyhocks and lilacs, or in gold
    at the opera,
Requires that one shall have lived so much! And not merely
Asking questions and giving answers, but grandly sitting,
Like a great rock, through many years.
It is the erratic path of time we trace
On the globe, with moist fingertip, and surely, the globe stops;
We are pointing to England, to Africa, to Nigeria;
And we shall visit these places, you and I, and other places,
Including heavenly Naples, queen of the sea, where I shall be king and
    you will be queen,
And all the places around Naples.
So the good old teacher is right, to stop with his finger on Naples, gazing

out into the mild December afternoon

As his star pupil enters the classroom in that elaborate black and yellow creation.

He is thinking of her flounces, and is caught in them as if they were made of iron, they will crush him to death!

Goodbye, old teacher, we must travel on, not to a better land, perhaps,

But to the England of the sonnets, Paris, Colombia, and Switzerland

And all the places with names, that we wish to visit—

Strasbourg, Albania,

The coast of Holland, Madrid, Singapore, Naples, Salonika, Liberia, and Turkey.

So we leave you behind with her of the black and yellow flounces.

You were always a good friend, but a special one.

Now as we brush through the clinging leaves we seem to hear you crying;

You want us to come back, but it is too late to come back, isn't it?

It is too late to go to the places with the names (what were they, anyway? just names).

It is too late to go anywhere but to the nearest star, that one, that hangs just over the hill, beckoning

Like a hand of which the arm is not visible. Goodbye, Father! Goodbye, pupils. Goodbye, my master and my dame.

We fly to the nearest star, whether it be red like a furnace, or yellow,

And we carry your lessons in our hearts (the lessons and our hearts are the same)

Out of the humid classroom, into the forever. Goodbye, Old Dog Tray.

And so they have left us feeling tired and old.

They never cared for school anyway.

And they have left us with the things pinned on the bulletin board,

And the night, the endless, muggy night that is invading our school.

HE

He cuts down the lakes so they appear straight
He smiles at his feet in their tired mules.
He turns up the music much louder.
He takes down the vaseline from the pantry shelf.

He is the capricious smile behind the colored bottles.
He eats not lest the poor want some.
He breathes of attitudes the piney altitudes.
He indeed is the White Cliffs of Dover.

He knows that his neck is frozen.
He snorts in the vale of dim wolves.
He writes to say, "If ever you visit this island,
He'll grow you back to your childhood.

"He is the liar behind the hedge
He grew one morning out of candor.
He is his own consolation prize.
He has had his eye on you from the beginning."

He hears the weak cut down with a smile.
He waltzes tragically on the spitting housetops.
He is never near. What you need
He cancels with the air of one making a salad.

He is always the last to know.
He is strength you once said was your bonnet.
He has appeared in "Carmen."
He is after us. If you decide

He is important, it will get you nowhere.
He is the source of much bitter reflection.
He used to be pretty for a rat.
He is now over-proud of his Etruscan appearance.

He walks in his sleep into your life.
He is worth knowing only for the children
He has reared as savages in Utah.
He helps his mother take in the clothes-line.

He is unforgettable as a shooting star.
He is known as "Liverlips."
He will tell you he has had a bad time of it.
He will try to pretend his pressagent is a temptress.

He looks terrible on the stairs.
He cuts himself on what he eats.
He was last seen flying to New York.
He was handing out cards which read:

"He wears a question in his left eye.
He dislikes the police but will associate with them.
He will demand something not on the menu.
He is invisible to the eyes of beauty and culture.

"He prevented the murder of Mistinguett in Mexico.
He has a knack for abortions. If you see
He is following you, forget him immediately:
He is dangerous even though asleep and unarmed."

A LONG NOVEL

What will his crimes become, now that her hands
Have gone to sleep? He gathers deeds

In the pure air, the agent
Of their factual excesses. He laughs as she inhales.

If it could have ended before
It began—the sorrow, the snow

Dropping, dropping its fine regrets.
The myrtle dries about his lavish brow.

He stands quieter than the day, a breath
In which all evils are one.

He is the purest air. But her patience,
The imperative Become, trembles

Where hands have been before. In the foul air
Each snowflake seems a Piranesi

Dropping in the past; his words are heavy
With their final meaning. Milady! Mimosa! So the end

Was the same: the discharge of spittle
Into frozen air. Except that, in a new

Humorous landscape, without music,
Written by music, he knew he was a saint,

While she touched all goodness
As golden hair, knowing its goodness

Impossible, and waking and waking
As it grew in the eyes of the beloved.

THE PIED PIPER

Under the day's crust a half-eaten child
And further sores which eyesight shall reveal
And they live. But what of dark elders
Whose touch at nightfall must now be
To keep their promise? Misery
Starches the host's one bed, his hand
Falls like an axe on her curls:
"Come in, come in! Better that the winter
Blaze unseen, than we two sleep apart!"

Who in old age will often part
From single sleep at the murmur
Of acerb revels under the hill;
Whose children couple as the earth crumbles
In vanity forever going down
A sunlit road, for his love was strongest
Who never loved them at all, and his notes
Most civil, laughing not to return.

LE LIVRE EST SUR LA TABLE

I
All beauty, resonance, integrity,
Exist by deprivation or logic
Of strange position. This being so,

We can only imagine a world in which a woman
Walks and wears her hair and knows
All that she does not know. Yet we know

What her breasts are. And we give fullness
To the dream. The table supports the book,
The plume leaps in the hand. But what

Dismal scene is this? The old man pouting
At a black cloud, the woman gone
Into the house, from which the wailing starts?

II
The young man places a bird-house
Against the blue sea. He walks away
And it remains. Now other

Men appear, but they live in boxes.
The sea protects them like a wall.
The gods worship a line-drawing

Of a woman, in the shadow of the sea
Which goes on writing. Are there
Collisions, communications on the shore

Or did all secrets vanish when
The woman left? Is the bird mentioned
In the waves' minutes, or did the land advance?

From
*THE
TENNIS
COURT
OATH*

THOUGHTS OF A YOUNG GIRL

"It is such a beautiful day I had to write you a letter
From the tower, and to show I'm not mad:
I only slipped on the cake of soap of the air
And drowned in the bathtub of the world.
You were too good to cry much over me.
And now I let you go. Signed, The Dwarf."

I passed by late in the afternoon
And the smile still played about her lips
As it has for centuries. She always knows
How to be utterly delightful. Oh my daughter,
My sweetheart, daughter of my late employer, princess,
May you not be long on the way!

"HOW MUCH LONGER WILL I BE ABLE
TO INHABIT THE DIVINE SEPULCHER . . ."

How much longer will I be able to inhabit the divine sepulcher
Of life, my great love? Do dolphins plunge bottomward
To find the light? Or is it rock
That is searched? Unrelentingly? Huh. And if some day

Men with orange shovels come to break open the rock
Which encases me, what about the light that comes in then?
What about the smell of the light?
What about the moss?

In pilgrim times he wounded me
Since then I only lie
My bed of light is a furnace choking me
With hell (and sometimes I hear salt water dripping).

I mean it—because I'm one of the few
To have held my breath under the house. I'll trade
One red sucker for two blue ones. I'm
Named Tom. The

Light bounces off mossy rocks down to me
In this glen (the neat villa! which
When he'd had he would not had he of
And jests under the smarting of privet

Which on hot spring nights perfumes the empty rooms
With the smell of sperm flushed down toilets
On hot summer afternoons within sight of the sea.
If you knew why then professor) reads

To his friends: Drink to me only with
And the reader is carried away
By a great shadow under the sea.
Behind the steering wheel

The boy took out his own forehead.
His girlfriend's head was a green bag
Of narcissus stems. "OK you win
But meet me anyway at Cohen's Drug Store

In 22 minutes." What a marvel is ancient man!
Under the tulip roots he has figured out a way to be a religious animal
And would be a mathematician. But where in unsuitable heaven
Can he get the heat that will make him grow?

For he needs something or will forever remain a dwarf,
Though a perfect one, and possessing a normal-sized brain
But he has got to be released by giants from things.
And as the plant grows older it realizes it will never be a tree,

Will probably always be haunted by a bee
And cultivates stupid impressions
So as not to become part of the dirt. The dirt
Is mounting like a sea. And we say goodbye

Shaking hands in front of the crashing of the waves
That give our words lonesomeness, and make these flabby hands
  seem ours—
Hands that are always writing things
On mirrors for people to see later—

Do you want them to water
Plant, tear listlessly among the exchangeable ivy—
Carrying food to mouth, touching genitals—
But no doubt you have understood

It all now and I am a fool. It remains
For me to get better, and to understand you so

Like a chair-sized man. Boots
Were heard on the floor above. In the garden the sunlight was still purple

But what buzzed in it had changed slightly
But not forever . . . but casting its shadow
On sticks, and looking around for an opening in the air, was quite as if it
    had never refused to exist differently. Guys
In the yard handled the belt he had made

Stars
Painted the garage roof crimson and black
He is not a man
Who can read these signs . . . his bones were stays . . .

And even refused to live
In a world and refunded the hiss
Of all that exists terribly near us
Like you, my love, and light.

For what is obedience but the air around us
To the house? For which the federal men came
In a minute after the sidewalk
Had taken you home? ("Latin . . . blossom . . .")

After which you led me to water
And bade me drink, which I did, owing to your kindness.
You would not let me out for two days and three nights,
Bringing me books bound in wild thyme and scented wild grasses

As if reading had any interest for me, you . . .
Now you are laughing.
Darkness interrupts my story.
Turn on the light.

Meanwhile what am I going to do?
I am growing up again, in school, the crisis will be very soon.
And you twist the darkness in your fingers, you
Who are slightly older . . .

Who are you, anyway?
And it is the color of sand,
The darkness, as it sifts through your hand
Because what does anything mean,

The ivy and the sand? That boat
Pulled up on the shore? Am I wonder,
Strategically, and in the light
Of the long sepulcher that hid death and hides me?

WHITE ROSES

The worst side of it all—
The white sunlight on the polished floor—
Pressed into service,
And then the window closed
And the night ends and begins again.
Her face goes green, her eyes are green,
In the dark corner playing "The Stars and Stripes Forever." I try to
    describe for you,
But you will not listen, you are like the swan.

No stars are there,
No stripes,
But a blind man's cane poking, however clumsily, into the inmost
    corners of the house.
Nothing can be harmed! Night and day are beginning again!
So put away the book,
The flowers you were keeping to give someone:
Only the white, tremendous foam of the street has any importance,
The new white flowers that are beginning to shoot up about now.

OUR YOUTH

Of bricks . . . Who built it? Like some crazy balloon
When love leans on us
Its nights . . . The velvety pavement sticks to our feet.
The dead puppies turn us back on love.

Where we are. Sometimes
The brick arches led to a room like a bubble, that broke when you
    entered it
And sometimes to a fallen leaf.
We got crazy with emotion, showing how much we knew.

The Arabs took us. We knew
The dead horses. We were discovering coffee,
How it is to be drunk hot, with bare feet
In Canada. And the immortal music of Chopin

Which we had been discovering for several months
Since we were fourteen years old. And coffee grounds,
And the wonder of hands, and the wonder of the day
When the child discovers her first dead hand.

Do you know it? Hasn't she
Observed you too? Haven't you been observed to her?
My, haven't the flowers been? Is the evil
In't? What window? What did you say there?

Heh? Eh? Our youth is dead.
From the minute we discover it with eyes closed
Advancing into mountain light.
Ouch . . . You will never have that young boy,

That boy with the monocle
Could have been your father

He is passing by. No, that other one,
Upstairs. He is the one who wanted to see you.

He is dead. Green and yellow handkerchiefs cover him.
Perhaps he will never rot, I see
That my clothes are dry. I will go.
The naked girl crosses the street.

Blue hampers . . . Explosions,
Ice . . . The ridiculous
Vases of porphyry. All that our youth
Can't use, that it was created for.

It's true we have not avoided our destiny
By weeding out the old people.
Our faces have filled with smoke. We escape
Down the cloud ladder, but the problem has not been solved.

AN ADDITIONAL POEM

Where then shall hope and fear their objects find?
The harbor cold to the mating ships,
And you have lost as you stand by the balcony
With the forest of the sea calm and gray beneath.
A strong impression torn from the descending light
But night is guilty. You knew the shadow
In the trunk was raving
But as you keep growing hungry you forget.
The distant box is open. A sound of grain
Poured over the floor in some eagerness—we
Rise with the night let out of the box of wind.

FAUST

If only the phantom would stop reappearing!
Business, if you wanted to know, was punk at the opera.
The heroine no longer appeared in *Faust*.
The crowds strolled sadly away. The phantom
Watched them from the roof, not guessing the hungers
That must be stirred before disappointment can begin,

One day as morning was about to begin
A man in brown with a white shirt reappearing
At the bottom of his yellow vest, was talking hungers
With the silver-haired director of the opera.
On the green-carpeted floor no phantom
Appeared, except yellow squares of sunlight, like those in *Faust*.

That night as the musicians for *Faust*
Were about to go on strike, lest darkness begin
In the corridors, and through them the phantom
Glide unobstructed, the vision reappearing
Of blonde Marguerite practicing a new opera
At her window awoke terrible new hungers

In the already starving tenor. But hungers
Are just another topic, like the new Faust
Drifting through the tunnels of the opera
(In search of lost old age? For they begin
To notice a twinkle in his eye. It is cold daylight reappearing
At the window behind him, itself a phantom

Window, painted by the phantom
Scene painters, sick of not getting paid, of hungers
For a scene below of tiny, reappearing
Dancers, with a sandbag falling like a note in *Faust*
Through purple air. And the spectators begin
To understand the bleeding tenor star of the opera.)

That night the opera
Was crowded to the rafters. The phantom
Took twenty-nine curtain calls. "Begin!
Begin!" In the wings the tenor hungers
For the heroine's convulsive kiss, and Faust
Moves forward, no longer young, reappearing

And reappearing for the last time. The opera
Faust would no longer need its phantom.
On the bare, sunlit stage the hungers could begin.

A LAST WORLD

These wonderful things
Were planted on the surface of a round mind that was to become our
   present time.
The mark of things belongs to someone
But if that somebody was wise
Then the whole of things might be different
From what it was thought to be in the beginning, before an angel bandaged
   the field glasses.
Then one could say nothing hear nothing
Of what the great time spoke to its divisors.
All borders between men were closed.
Now all is different without having changed
As though one were to pass through the same street at different times
And nothing that is old can prefer the new.
An enormous merit has been placed on the head of all things
Which, bowing down, arrive near the region of their feet
So that the earth-stone has stared at them in memory at the approach of an
   error.
Still it is not too late for these things to die
Provided that an anemone will grab them and rush them to the wildest
   heaven.
But having plucked oneself, who could live in the sunlight?
And the truth is cold, as a giant's knee
Will seem cold.

Yet having once played with tawny truth
Having once looked at a cold mullet on a plate on a table supported by the
   weight of the inconstant universe
He wished to go far away from himself.
There were no baskets in those jovial pine-tree forests, and the waves
   pushed without whitecaps
In that foam where he wished to be.

Man is never without woman, the neuter sex
Casting up her equations, looks to her lord for loving kindness
For man smiles never at woman.
In the forests a night landslide could disclose that she smiled.
Guns were fired to discourage dogs into the interior
But woman—never. She is completely out of this world.
She climbs a tree to see if he is coming
Sunlight breaks at the edges of the wet lakes
And she is happy, if free
For the power he forces down at her like a storm of lightning.

Once a happy old man
One can never change the core of things, and light burns you the harder
    for it.
Glad of the changes already and if there are more it will never be you
    that minds
Since it will not be you to be changed, but in the evening in the severe
    lamplight doubts come
From many scattered distances, and do not come too near.
As it falls along the house, your treasure
Cries to the other men; the darkness will have none of you, and you are
    folded into it like mint into the sound of haying.
It was ninety-five years ago that you strolled in the serene little port; under
    an enormous cornice six boys in black slowly stood.
Six frock coats today, six black fungi tomorrow,
And the day after tomorrow—but the day after tomorrow itself is
    blackening dust.
You court obsidian pools
And from a tremendous height twilight falls like a stone and hits you.

You who were always in the way
Flower
Are you afraid of trembling like breath

But there is no breath in seriousness; the lake howls for it.
Swiftly sky covers earth, the wrong breast for a child to suck, and that,
What have you got there in your hand?
It is a stone

So the passions are divided into tiniest units
And of these many are lost, and those that remain are given at nightfall to
  the uneasy old man
The old man who goes skipping along the roadbed.
In a dumb harvest
Passions are locked away, and states of creation are used instead, that is to
  say synonyms are used.

Honey
On the lips of elders is not contenting, so
A firebrand is made. Woman carries it,
She who thought herself good only for bearing children is decked out in the
  lace of fire
And this is exactly the way she wanted it, the trees coming to place
  themselves in her
In a rite of torpor, dust.
A bug carries the elixir
Naked men pray the ground and chew it with their hands
The fire lives
Men are nabbed
She her bonnet half off is sobbing there while the massacre yet
  continues with a terrific thin energy
A silver blaze calms the darkness.

Rest undisturbed on the dry of the beach
Flower
And night stand suddenly sideways to observe your bones
Vixen

Do men later go home
Because we wanted to travel
Under the kettle of trees
We thought the sky would melt to see us
But to tell the truth the air turned to smoke,
We were forced back onto a foul pillow that was another place.
Or were lost by our comrades
Somewhere between heaven and no place, and were growing smaller.
In another place a mysterious mist shot up like a wall, down which trickled
    the tears of our loved ones.
Bananas rotten with their ripeness hung from the leaves, and cakes and
    jewels covered the sand.
But these were not the best men
But there were moments of the others
Seen through indifference, only bare methods
But we can remember them and so we are saved.

A last world moves on the figures;
They are smaller than when we last saw them caring about them.
The sky is a giant rocking horse
And of the other things death is a new office building filled with modern
    furniture,
A wise thing, but which has no purpose for us.

Everything is being blown away;
A little horse trots up with a letter in its mouth, which is read with
    eagerness
As we gallop into the flame.

From *THE NEW REALISM*

There was calm rapture in the way she spoke
Perhaps I would get over the way the joke
Always turned against me, in the end.
The bars had been removed from all the windows
There was something quiet in the way the light entered
Her trousseau. Wine fished out of the sea—they hadn't known
We were coming relaxed forever
We stood off the land because if you get too far
From a perfume you can squeeze the life out of it
One seal came into view and then the others
Yellow in the vast sun.
A watchdog performed and they triumphed
The day was bleak—ice had replaced air
The sigh of the children to former music
Supplanting the mutt's yelps.
This was as far as she would go—
A tavern with plants.
Dynamite out over the horizon
And a sequel, and a racket. Dolphins repelling
The sand. Squads of bulldozers
Wrecked the site, and she died laughing
Because only once does prosperity let you get away
On your doorstep she used to explain
How if the returning merchants in the morning hitched the rim of the van
In the evening one must be very quick to give them the slip.
The judge knocked. The zinnias
Had never looked better—red, yellow, and blue
They were, and the forget-me-nots and dahlias
At least sixty different varieties
As the shade went up
And the ambulance came crashing through the dust
Of the new day, the moon and the sun and the stars,
And the iceberg slowly sank
In the volcano and the sea ran far away
Yellow over the hot sand, green as the green trees.

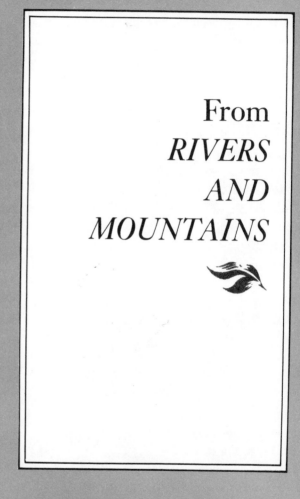

From
*RIVERS
AND
MOUNTAINS*

RIVERS AND MOUNTAINS

On the secret map the assassins
Cloistered, the Moon River was marked
Near the eighteen peaks and the city
Of humiliation and defeat—wan ending
Of the trail among dry, papery leaves
Gray-brown quills like thoughts
In the melodious but vast mass of today's
Writing through fields and swamps
Marked, on the map, with little bunches of weeds.
Certainly squirrels lived in the woods
But devastation and dull sleep still
Hung over the land, quelled
The rioters turned out of sleep in the peace of prisons
Singing on marble factory walls
Deaf consolation of minor tunes that pack
The air with heavy invisible rods
Pent in some sand valley from
Which only quiet walking ever instructs.
The bird flew over and
Sat—there was nothing else to do.
Do not mistake its silence for pride or strength
Or the waterfall for a harbor
Full of light boats that is there
Performing for thousands of people
In clothes some with places to go
Or games. Sometimes over the pillar
Of square stones its impact
Makes a light print.

So going around cities
To get to other places you found
It all on paper but the land
Was made of paper processed
To look like ferns, mud or other

Whose sea unrolled its magic
Distances and then rolled them up
Its secret was only a pocket
After all but some corners are darker
Than these moonless nights spent as on a raft
In the seclusion of a melody heard
As though through trees
And you can never ignite their touch
Long but there were homes
Flung far out near the asperities
Of a sharp, rocky pinnacle
And other collective places
Shadows of vineyards whose wine
Tasted of the forest floor
Fisheries and oyster beds
Tides under the pole
Seminaries of instruction, public
Places for electric light
And the major tax assessment area
Wrinkled on the plan
Of election to public office
Sixty-two years old bath and breakfast
The formal traffic, shadows
To make it not worth joining
After the ox had pulled away the cart.

Your plan was to separate the enemy into two groups
With the razor-edged mountains between.
It worked well on paper
But their camp had grown
To be the mountains and the map
Carefully peeled away and not torn
Was the light, a tender but tough bark
On everything. Fortunately the war was solved

In another way by isolating the two sections
Of the enemy's navy so that the mainland
Warded away the big floating ships.
Light bounced off the ends
Of the small gray waves to tell
Them in the observatory
About the great drama that was being won
To turn off the machinery
And quietly move among the rustic landscape
Scooping snow off the mountains rinsing
The coarser ones that love had
Slowly risen in the night to overflow
Wetting pillow and petal
Determined to place the letter
On the unassassinated president's desk
So that a stamp could reproduce all this
In detail, down to the last autumn leaf
And the affliction of June ride
Slowly out into the sun-blackened landscape.

LAST MONTH

No changes of support—only
Patches of gray, here where sunlight fell.
The house seems heavier
Now that they have gone away.
In fact it emptied in record time.
When the flat table used to result
A match recedes, slowly, into the night.
The academy of the future is
Opening its doors and willing
The fruitless sunlight streams into domes,
The chairs piled high with books and papers.

The sedate one is this month's skittish one
Confirming the property that,
A timeless value, has changed hands.
And you could have a new automobile
Ping pong set and garage, but the thief
Stole everything like a miracle.
In his book there was a picture of treason only
And in the garden, cries and colors.

IF THE BIRDS KNEW

It is better this year.
And the clothes they wear
In the gray unweeded sky of our earth
There is no possibility of change
Because all of the true fragments are here.
So I was glad of the fog's
Taking me to you
Undetermined summer thing eaten
Of grief and passage—where you stay.
The wheel is ready to turn again.
When you have gone it will light up,
The shadow of the spokes to drown
Your departure where the summer knells
Speak to grown dawn.
There is after all a kind of promise
To the affair of the waiting weather.
We have learned not to be tired
Among the lanterns of this year of sleep
But someone pays—no transparency
Has ever hardened us before
To long piers of silence, and hedges
Of understanding, difficult passing
From one lesson to the next and the coldness
Of the consistency of our lives'
Devotion to immaculate danger.
A leaf would have settled the disturbance
Of the atmosphere, but at that high
Valley's point disbanded
Clouds that rocks smote newly
The person or persons involved
Parading slowly through the sunlit fields
Not only as though the danger did not exist
But as though the birds were in on the secret.

INTO THE DUSK-CHARGED AIR

Far from the Rappahannock, the silent
Danube moves along toward the sea.
The brown and green Nile rolls slowly
Like the Niagara's welling descent.
Tractors stood on the green banks of the Loire
Near where it joined the Cher.
The St. Lawrence prods among black stones
And mud. But the Arno is all stones.
Wind ruffles the Hudson's
Surface. The Irawaddy is overflowing.
But the yellowish, gray Tiber
Is contained within steep banks. The Isar
Flows too fast to swim in, the Jordan's water
Courses over the flat land. The Allegheny and its boats
Were dark blue. The Moskowa is
Gray boats. The Amstel flows slowly.
Leaves fall into the Connecticut as it passes
Underneath. The Liffey is full of sewage,
Like the Seine, but unlike
The brownish-yellow Dordogne.
Mountains hem in the Colorado
And the Oder is very deep, almost
As deep as the Congo is wide.
The plain banks of the Neva are
Gray. The dark Saône flows silently.
And the Volga is long and wide
As it flows across the brownish land. The Ebro
Is blue, and slow. The Shannon flows
Swiftly between its banks. The Mississippi
Is one of the world's longest rivers, like the Amazon.
It has the Missouri for a tributary.
The Harlem flows amid factories
And buildings. The Nelson is in Canada,
Flowing. Through hard banks the Dubawnt

Forces its way. People walk near the Trent.
The landscape around the Mohawk stretches away;
The Rubicon is merely a brook.
In winter the Main
Surges; the Rhine sings its eternal song.
The Rhône slogs along through whitish banks
And the Rio Grande spins tales of the past.
The Loir bursts its frozen shackles
But the Moldau's wet mud ensnares it.
The East catches the light.
Near the Escaut the noise of factories echoes
And the sinuous Humboldt gurgles wildly.
The Po too flows, and the many-colored
Thames. Into the Atlantic Ocean
Pours the Garonne. Few ships navigate
On the Housatonic, but quite a few can be seen
On the Elbe. For centuries
The Afton has flowed.
                              If the Rio Negro
Could abandon its song, and the Magdalena
The jungle flowers, the Tagus
Would still flow serenely, and the Ohio
Abrade its slate banks. The tan Euphrates would
Sidle silently across the world. The Yukon
Was choked with ice, but the Susquehanna still pushed
Bravely along. The Dee caught the day's last flares
Like the Pilcomayo's carrion rose.
The Peace offered eternal fragrance
Perhaps, but the Mackenzie churned livid mud
Like tan chalk-marks. Near where
The Brahmaputra slapped swollen dikes
Was an opening through which the Limmat
Could have trickled. A young man strode the Churchill's
Banks, thinking of night. The Vistula seized

The shadows. The Theiss, stark mad, bubbled
In the windy evening. And the Ob shuffled
Crazily along. Fat billows encrusted the Dniester's
Pallid flood, and the Fraser's porous surface.
Fish gasped amid the Spree's reeds. A boat
Descended the bobbing Orinoco. When the
Marne flowed by the plants nodded
And above the glistering Gila
A sunset as beautiful as the Athabasca
Stammered. The Zambezi chimed. The Oxus
Flowed somewhere. The Paranaíba
Is flowing, like the wind-washed Cumberland.
The Araguaia flows in the rain.
And, through overlying rocks the Isère
Cascades gently. The Guadalquivir sputtered.
Someday time will confound the Indre,
Making a rill of the Huang Ho. And
The Potomac rumbles softly. Crested birds
Watch the Ucayali go
Through dreaming night. You cannot stop
The Yenisei. And afterwards
The White flows strongly to its . . .
Goal. If the Tyne's shores
Hold you, and the Albany
Arrest your development, can you resist the Red's
Musk, the Meuse's situation?
A particle of mud in the Neckar
Does not turn it black. You cannot
Like the Saskatchewan, nor refuse
The meandering Yangtze, unleash
The Genesee. Does the Scamander
Still irrigate crimson plains? And the Durance
And the Pechora? The São Francisco
Skulks amid gray, rubbery nettles. The Liard's

Reflexes are slow, and the Arkansas erodes
Anthracite hummocks. The Paraná stinks.
The Ottawa is light emerald green
Among grays. Better that the Indus fade
In steaming sands! Let the Brazos
Freeze solid! And the Wabash turn to a leaden
Cinder of ice! The Marañón is too tepid, we must
Find a way to freeze it hard. The Ural
Is freezing slowly in the blasts. The black Yonne
Congeals nicely. And the Petit-Morin
Curls up on the solid earth. The Inn
Does not remember better times, and the Merrimack's
Galvanized. The Ganges is liquid snow by now;
The Vyatka's ice-gray. The once-molten Tennessee's
Curdled. The Japurá is a pack of ice. Gelid
The Columbia's gray loam banks. The Don's merely
A giant icicle. The Niger freezes, slowly.
The interminable Lena plods on
But the Purus' mercurial waters are icy, grim
With cold. The Loing is choked with fragments of ice.
The Weser is frozen, like liquid air.
And so is the Kama. And the beige, thickly flowing
Tocantins. The rivers bask in the cold.
The stern Uruguay chafes its banks,
A mass of ice. The Hooghly is solid
Ice. The Adour is silent, motionless.
The lovely Tigris is nothing but scratchy ice
Like the Yellowstone, with its osier-clustered banks.
The Mekong is beginning to thaw out a little
And the Donets gurgles beneath the
Huge blocks of ice. The Manzanares gushes free.
The Illinois darts through the sunny air again.
But the Dnieper is still ice-bound. Somewhere
The Salado propels its floes, but the Roosevelt's

Frozen. The Oka is frozen solider
Than the Somme. The Minho slumbers
In winter, nor does the Snake
Remember August. Hilarious, the Canadian
Is solid ice. The Madeira slavers
Across the thawing fields, and the Plata laughs.
The Dvina soaks up the snow. The Sava's
Temperature is above freezing. The Avon
Carols noiselessly. The Drôme presses
Grass banks; the Adige's frozen
Surface is like gray pebbles.

Birds circle the Ticino. In winter
The Var was dark blue, unfrozen. The
Thwaite, cold, is choked with sandy ice;
The Ardèche glistens feebly through the freezing rain.

THE ECCLESIAST

"Worse than the sunflower," she had said.
But the new dimension of truth had only recently
Burst in on us. Now it was to be condemned.
And in vagrant shadow her mothball truth is eaten.
In cool, like-it-or-not shadow the humdrum is consumed.
Tired housewives begat it some decades ago,
A small piece of truth that if it was honey to the lips
Was also millions of miles from filling the place reserved for it.
You see how honey crumbles your universe
Which seems like an institution—how many walls?

Then everything, in her belief, was to be submerged
And soon. There was no life you could live out to its end
And no attitude which, in the end, would save you.
The monkish and the frivolous alike were to be trapped
    in death's capacious claw
But listen while I tell you about the wallpaper—
There was a key to everything in that oak forest
But a sad one. Ever since childhood there
Has been this special meaning to everything.
You smile at your friend's joke, but only later, through tears.

For the shoe pinches, even though it fits perfectly.
Apples were made to be gathered, also the whole host of the
    world's ailments and troubles.
There is no time like the present for giving in to this temptation.
Tomorrow you'll weep—what of it? There is time enough
Once the harvest is in and the animals put away for the winter
To stand at the uncomprehending window cultivating the desert
With salt tears which will never do anyone any good.
My dearest I am as a galleon on salt billows.
Perfume my head with forgetting all about me.

For some day these projects will return.
The funereal voyage over ice-strewn seas is ended.
You wake up forgetting. Already
Daylight shakes you in the yard.
The hands remain empty. They are constructing an osier basket
Just now, and across the sunlight darkness is taking root anew
In intense activity. You shall never have seen it just this way
And that is to be your one reward.

Fine vapors escape from whatever is doing the living.
The night is cold and delicate and full of angels
Pounding down the living. The factories are all lit up,
The chime goes unheard.
We are together at last, though far apart.

THE RECENT PAST

Perhaps we ought to feel with more imagination.
As today the sky 70 degrees above zero with lines falling
The way September moves a lace curtain to be near a pear,
The oddest device can't be usual. And that is where
The pejorative sense of fear moves axles. In the stars
There is no longer any peace, emptied like a cup of coffee
Between the blinding rain that interviews.

You were my quintuplets when I decided to leave you
Opening a picture book the pictures were all of grass
Slowly the book was on fire, you the reader
Sitting with specs full of smoke exclaimed
How it was a rhyme for "brick" or "redder."
The next chapter told all about a brook.
You were beginning to see the relation when a tidal wave
Arrived with sinking ships that spelled out "Aladdin."
I thought about the Arab boy in his cave
But the thoughts came faster than advice.
If you knew that snow was a still toboggan in space
The print could rhyme with "fallen star."

A BLESSING IN DISGUISE

Yes, they are alive and can have those colors,
But I, in my soul, am alive too.
I feel I must sing and dance, to tell
Of this in a way, that knowing you may be drawn to me.

And I sing amid despair and isolation
Of the chance to know you, to sing of me
Which are you. You see,
You hold me up to the light in a way

I should never have expected, or suspected, perhaps
Because you always tell me I am you,
And right. The great spruces loom.
I am yours to die with, to desire.

I cannot ever think of me, I desire you
For a room in which the chairs ever
Have their backs turned to the light
Inflicted on the stone and paths, the real trees

That seem to shine at me through a lattice toward you.
If the wild light of this January day is true
I pledge me to be truthful unto you
Whom I cannot ever stop remembering.

Remembering to forgive. Remember to pass beyond you into the day
On the wings of the secret you will never know.
Taking me from myself, in the path
Which the pastel girth of the day has assigned to me.

I prefer "you" in the plural, I want "you,"
You must come to me, all golden and pale
Like the dew and the air.
And then I start getting this feeling of exaltation.

CLEPSYDRA

Hasn't the sky? Returned from moving the other
Authority recently dropped, wrested as much of
That severe sunshine as you need now on the way
You go. The reason why it happened only since
You woke up is letting the steam disappear
From those clouds when the landscape all around
Is hilly sites that will have to be reckoned
Into the total for there to be more air: that is,
More fitness read into the undeduced result, than land.
This means never getting any closer to the basic
Principle operating behind it than to the distracted
Entity of a mirage. The half-meant, half-perceived
Motions of fronds out of idle depths that are
Summer. And expansion into little draughts.
The reply wakens easily, darting from
Untruth to willed moment, scarcely called into being
Before it swells, the way a waterfall
Drums at different levels. Each moment
Of utterance is the true one; likewise none are true,
Only is the bounding from air to air, a serpentine
Gesture which hides the truth behind a congruent
Message, the way air hides the sky, is, in fact,
Tearing it limb from limb this very moment: but
The sky has pleaded already and this is about
As graceful a kind of non-absence as either
Has a right to expect: whether it's the form of
Some creator who has momentarily turned away,
Marrying detachment with respect, so that the pieces
Are seen as parts of a spectrum, independent
Yet symbolic of their staggered times of arrival;
Whether on the other hand all of it is to be
Seen as no luck. A recurring whiteness like
The face of stone pleasure, urging forward as
Nostrils what only meant dust. But the argument,

That is its way, has already left these behind: it
Is, it would have you believe, the white din up ahead
That matters: unformed yells, rocketings,
Affected turns, and tones of voice called
By upper shadows toward some cloud of belief
Or its unstated circumference. But the light
Has already gone from there too and it may be that
It is lines contracting into a plane. We hear so much
Of its further action that at last it seems that
It is we, our taking it into account rather, that are
The reply that prompted the question, and
That the latter, like a person waking on a pillow
Has the sensation of having dreamt the whole thing,
Of returning to participate in that dream, until
The last word is exhausted; certainly this is
Peace of a sort, like nets drying in the sun,
That we must progress toward the whole thing
About an hour ago. As long as it is there
You will desire it as its tag of wall sinks
Deeper as though hollowed by sunlight that
Just fits over it; it is both mirage and the little
That was present, the miserable totality
Mustered at any given moment, like your eyes
And all they speak of, such as your hands, in lost
Accents beyond any dream of ever wanting them again.
To have this to be constantly coming back from—
Nothing more, really, than surprise at your absence
And preparing to continue the dialogue into
Those mysterious and near regions that are
Precisely the time of its being furthered.
Seeing it, as it was, dividing that time,
Casting colored paddles against the welter
Of a future of disunion just to abolish confusion
And permit level walks into the gaze of its standing

Around admiringly, it was then, that it was these
Moments that were the truth, although each tapered
Into the distant surrounding night. But
Wasn't it their blindness, instead, and wasn't this
The fact of being so turned in on each other that
Neither would ever see his way clear again? It
Did not stagger the imagination so long as it stayed
This way, comparable to exclusion from the light of the stars
That drenched every instant of that being, in an egoistic way,
As though their round time were only the reverse
Of some more concealable, vengeful purpose to become known
Once its result had more or less established
The look of the horizon. But the condition
Of those moments of timeless elasticity and blindness
Was being joined secretly so
That their paths would cross again and be separated
Only to join again in a final assumption rising like a shout
And be endless in the discovery of the declamatory
Nature of the distance traveled. All this is
Not without small variations and surprises, yet
An invisible fountain continually destroys and refreshes the previsions.
Then is their permanence merely a function of
The assurance with which it's understood, assurance
Which, you might say, goes a long way toward conditioning
Whatever result? But there was no statement
At the beginning. There was only a breathless waste,
A dumb cry shaping everything in projected
After-effects orphaned by playing the part intended for them,
Though one must not forget that the nature of this
Emptiness, these previsions,
Was that it could only happen here, on this page held
Too close to be legible, sprouting erasures, except that they
Ended everything in the transparent sphere of what was
Intended only a moment ago, spiraling further out, its

Gesture finally dissolving in the weather.
It was the long way back out of sadness
Of that first meeting: a half-triumph, an imaginary feeling
Which still protected its events and pauses, the way
A telescope protects its view of distant mountains
And all they include, the coming and going,
Moving correctly up to other levels, preparing to spend the night
There where the tiny figures halt as darkness comes on,
Beside some loud torrent in an empty yet personal
Landscape, which has the further advantage of being
What surrounds without insisting, the very breath so
Honorably offered, and accepted in the same spirit.
There was in fact pleasure in those high walls.
Each moment seemed to bore back into the centuries
For profit and manners, and an old way of looking that
Continually shaped those lips into a smile. Or it was
Like standing at the edge of a harbor early on a summer morning
With the discreet shadows cast by the water all around
And a feeling, again, of emptiness, but of richness in the way
The whole thing is organized, on what a miraculous scale,
Really what is meant by a human level, with the figures of giants
Not too much bigger than the men who have come to petition them:
A moment that gave not only itself, but
Also the means of keeping it, of not turning to dust
Or gestures somewhere up ahead
But of becoming complicated like the torrent
In new dark passages, tears and laughter which
Are a sign of life, of distant life in this case.
And yet, as always happens, there would come a moment when
Acts no longer sufficed and the calm
Of this true progression hardened into shreds
Of another kind of calm, returning to the conclusion, its premises
Undertaken before any formal agreement had been reached, hence
A writ that was the shadow of the colossal reason behind all this

Like a second, rigid body behind the one you know is yours.
And it was in vain that tears blotted the contract now, because
It had been freely drawn up and consented to as insurance
Against the very condition it was now so efficiently
Seeking to establish. It had reduced that other world,
The round one of the telescope, to a kind of very fine powder or dust
So small that space could not remember it.
Thereafter any signs of feeling were cut short by
The comfort and security, a certain elegance even,
Like the fittings of a ship, that are after all
The most normal things in the world. Yes, perhaps, but the words
"After all" are important for understanding the almost
Exaggerated strictness of the condition, and why, in spite of this,
It seemed the validity of the former continuing was
Not likely to be reinstated for a long time.
"After all," that too might be possible, as indeed
All kinds of things are possible in the widening angle of
The day, as it comes to blush with pleasure and increase,
So that light sinks into itself, becomes dark and heavy
Like a surface stained with ink: there was something
Not quite good or correct about the way
Things were looking recently: hadn't the point
Of all this new construction been to provide
A protected medium for the exchanges each felt of such vital
Concern, and wasn't it now giving itself the airs of a palace?
And yet her hair had never been so long.
It was a feeling of well-being, if you will, as though a smallest
Distant impulse had rendered the whole surface ultra-sensitive
But its fierceness was still acquiescence
To the nature of this goodness already past
And it was a kind of sweet acknowledgment of how
The past is yours, to keep invisible if you wish
But also to make absurd elaborations with
And in this way prolong your dance of non-discovery

In brittle, useless architecture that is nevertheless
The map of your desires, irreproachable, beyond
Madness and the toe of approaching night, if only
You desire to arrange it this way. Your acts
Are sentinels against this quiet
Invasion. Long may you prosper, and may your years
Be the throes of what is even now exhausting itself
In one last effort to outwit us; it could only be a map
Of the world: in their defeat such peninsulas as become
Prolongations of our reluctance to approach, but also
Fine days on whose memorable successions of events
We shall be ever afterwards tempted to dwell. I am
Not speaking of a partially successful attempt to be
Opposite; anybody at all can read that page, it has only
To be thrust in front of him. I mean now something much broader,
The sum total of all the private aspects that can ever
Become legible in what is outside, as much in the rocks
And foliage as in the invisible look of the distant
Ether and in the iron fist that suddenly closes over your own.
I see myself in this totality, and meanwhile
I am only a transparent diagram, of manners and
Private words with the certainty of being about to fall.
And even this crumb of life I also owe to you
For being so close as to seal out knowledge of that other
Voluntary life, and so keep its root in darkness until your
Maturity when your hair will actually be the branches
Of a tree with the light pouring through them.
It intensifies echoes in such a way as to
Form a channel to absorb every correct motion.
In this way any direction taken was the right one,
Leading first to you, and through you to
Myself that is beyond you and which is the same thing as space,
That is the stammering vehicles that remain unknown,
Eating the sky in all sincerity because the difference

Can never be made up: therefore, why not examine the distance?
It seemed he had been repeating the same stupid phrase
Over and over throughout his life; meanwhile
Infant destinies had suavely matured; there was
To be a meeting or collection of them that very evening.
He was out of it of course for having lain happily awake
On the tepid fringes of that field or whatever
Whose center was beginning to churn darkly, but even more
   for having
The progression of minutes by accepting them, as one accepts
   drops of rain
As they form a shower, and without worrying about the fine
   weather that will come after.
Why shouldn't all climate and all music be equal
Without growing? There should be an invariable balance of
Contentment to hold everything in place, ministering
To stunted memories, helping them stand alone
And return into the world, without ever looking back at
What they might have become, even though in doing so they
Might just once have been the truth that, invisible,
Still surrounds us like the air and is the dividing force
Between our slightest steps and the notes taken on them.
It is because everything is relative
That we shall never see in that sphere of pure wisdom and
Entertainment much more than groping shadows of an incomplete
Former existence so close it burns like the mouth that
Closes down over all your effort like the moment
Of death, but stays, raging and burning the design of
Its intentions into the house of your brain, until
You wake up alone, the certainty that it
Wasn't a dream your only clue to why the walls
Are turning on you and why the windows no longer speak
Of time but are themselves, transparent guardians you
Invented for what there was to hide. Which has now

Grown up, or moved away, as a jewel
Exists when there is no one to look at it, and this
Existence saps your own. Perhaps you are being kept here
Only so that somewhere else the peculiar light of someone's
Purpose can blaze unexpectedly in the acute
Angles of the rooms. It is not a question, then,
Of having not lived in vain. What is meant is that this distant
Image of you, the way you really are, is the test
Of how you see yourself, and regardless of whether or not
You hesitate, it may be assumed that you have won, that this
Wooden and external representation
Returns the full echo of what you meant
With nothing left over, from that circumference now alight
With ex-possibilities become present fact, and you
Must wear them like clothing, moving in the shadow of
Your single and twin existence, waking in intact
Appreciation of it, while morning is still and before the body
Is changed by the faces of evening.

From *THE SKATERS*

From II
Old heavens, you used to tweak above us,
Standing like rain whenever a salvo . . . Old heavens,
You lying there above the old, but not ruined, fort,
Can you hear, there, what I am saying?

For it is you I am parodying,
Your invisible denials. And the almost correct impressions
Corroborated by newsprint, which is so fine.
I call to you there, but I do not think that you will answer me.

For I am condemned to drum my fingers
On the closed lid of this piano, this tedious planet, earth
As it winks to you through the aspiring, growing distances,
A last spark before the night.

There was much to be said in favor of storms
But you seem to have abandoned them in favor of endless light.
I cannot say that I think the change much of an improvement.
There is something fearful in these summer nights that go on forever. . . .

We are nearing the Moorish coast, I think, in a *bateau*.
I wonder if I will have any friends there
Whether the future will be kinder to me than the past, for example,
And am all set to be put out, finding it to be not.

Still, I am prepared for this voyage, and for anything else you may care to
    mention.
Not that I am not afraid, but there is very little time left.
You have probably made travel arrangements, and know the feeling.
Suddenly, one morning, the little train arrives in the station, but oh, so big

It is! Much bigger and faster than anyone told you.

A bearded student in an old baggy overcoat is waiting to take it.

"Why do you want to go *there*," they all say. "It is better in the
other direction."

And so it is. There people are free, at any rate. But where you are
going no one is.

Still there are parks and libraries to be visited, "la Bibliothèque
Municipale,"

Hotel reservations and all that rot. Old American films dubbed into the
foreign language,

Coffee and whiskey and cigar stubs. Nobody minds. And rain on the
bristly wool of your topcoat.

I realize that I never knew why I wanted to come.

Yet I shall never return to the past, that attic.

Its sailboats are perhaps more beautiful than these, these I am leaning
against,

Spangled with diamonds and orange and purple stains,

Bearing me once again in quest of the unknown. These sails are life itself
to me.

I heard a girl say this once, and cried, and brought her fresh fruit and
fishes,

Olives and golden baked loaves. She dried her tears and thanked me.

Now we are both setting sail into the purplish evening.

I love it! This cruise can never last long enough for me.

But once more, office desks, radiators—No! That is behind me.

No more dullness, only movies and love and laughter, sex and fun.

The ticket seller is blowing his little horn—hurry before the window
slams down.

The train we are getting onto is a boat train, and the boats are really boats
this time.

But I heard the heavens say—Is it right? This continual changing back
   and forth?
Laughter and tears and so on? Mightn't just plain sadness be sufficient for
   him?
No! I'll not accept that any more, you bewhiskered old caverns of blue!
This is just right for me. I am cozily ensconced in the balcony of my face

Looking out over the whole darn countryside, a beacon of satisfaction
I am. I'll not trade places with a king. Here I am then, continuing but ever
   beginning
My perennial voyage, into new memories, new hope and flowers
The way the coasts glide past you. I shall never forget this moment

Because it consists of purest ecstasy. I am happier now than I ever dared
   believe
Anyone could be. And we finger down the dog-eared coasts. . . .
It is all passing! It is past! No, I am here,
Bellow the coasts, and even the heavens roar their assent

As we pick up a lemon-colored light horizontally
Projected into the night, the night that heaven
Was kind enough to send, and I launch into the happiest dreams,
Happier once again, because tomorrow is already here.

Yet certain kernels remain. Clouds that drift past sheds—
Read it in the official bulletin. We shan't be putting out today.
The old stove smoked worse than ever because rain was coming down its
   chimney.
Only the bleary eye of fog accosted one through the mended pane.

Outside, the swamp water lapped the broken wood step.
A rowboat was moored in the alligator-infested swamp.

Somewhere, from deep in the interior of the jungle, a groan was heard.
Could it be . . . ? Anyway, a rainy day—wet weather.

The whole voyage will have to be canceled.
It would be impossible to make different connections.
Besides, the hotels are all full at this season. The junks packed with
  refugees
Returning from the islands. Sea-bream and flounder abound in the
  muddied waters. . . .

They in fact represent the backbone of the island economy.
That, and cigar rolling. Please leave your papers at the desk as you pass
  out,
You know. "The Wedding March." Ah yes, that's the way. The couple
  descend
The steps of the little old church. Ribbons are flung, ribbons of cloud

And the sun seems to be coming out. But there have been so many false
  alarms. . . .
No, it's happened! The storm is over. Again the weather is fine and clear.
And the voyage? It's on! Listen everybody, the ship is starting,
I can hear its whistle's roar! We have just time enough to make it to the
  dock!

And away they pour, in the sulfurous sunlight,
To the aqua and silver waters where stands the glistening white ship
And into the great vessel they flood, a motley and happy crowd
Chanting and pouring down hymns on the surface of the ocean. . . .

Pulling, tugging us along with them, by means of streamers,
Golden and silver confetti. Smiling, we laugh and sing with the
  revelers

But are not quite certain that we want to go—the dock is so sunny and
    warm.
That majestic ship will pull up anchor who knows where?

And full of laughter and tears, we sidle once again with the other
    passengers.
The ground is heaving under foot. Is it the ship? It could be the dock. . . .
And with a great whoosh all the sails go up. . . . Hideous black smoke
    belches forth from the funnels
Smudging the gold carnival costumes with the gaiety of its jet-black soot

And, as into a tunnel the voyage starts
Only, as I said, to be continued. The eyes of those left standing on the
    dock are wet
But ours are dry. Into the secretive, vaporous night with all of us!
Into the unknown, the unknown that loves us, the great unknown!

IV
The wind thrashes the maple seed-pods,
The whole brilliant mass comes spattering down.

This is my fourteenth year as governor of C province.
I was little more than a lad when I first came here.
Now I am old but scarcely any wiser.
So little are white hair and a wrinkled forehead a sign of wisdom!

To slowly raise oneself
Hand over hand, lifting one's entire weight;
To forget there was a possibility
Of some more politic movement. That freedom, courage
And pleasant company could exist.
That has always been behind you.

An earlier litigation: wind hard in the tops
Of the baggy eucalyptus branches.

Today I wrote, "The spring is late this year.
In the early mornings there is hoarfrost on the water meadows.
And on the highway the frozen ruts are papered over with ice."

The day was gloves.

How far from the usual statement
About time, ice—the weather itself had gone.

I mean this. Through the years
You have approached an inventory
And it is now that tomorrow
Is going to be the climax of your casual
Statement about yourself, begun
So long ago in humility and false quietude.

The sands are frantic
In the hourglass. But there is time
To change, to utterly destroy
That too-familiar image
Lurking in the glass
Each morning, at the edge of the mirror.

The train is still sitting in the station.
You only dreamed it was in motion.

There are a few travelers on Z high road.
Behind a shutter, two black eyes are watching them.
They belong to the wife of P, the high-school principal.

The screen door bangs in the wind, one of the hinges is loose.
And together we look back at the house.
It could use a coat of paint
Except that I am too poor to hire a workman.

I have all I can do to keep body and soul together
And soon, even that relatively simple task may prove to be beyond my
    powers.

That was a good joke you played on the other guests.
A joke of silence.

One seizes these moments as they come along, afraid
To believe too much in the happiness that might result
Or confide too much of one's love and fear, even in
Oneself.

The spring, though mild, is incredibly wet.
I have spent the afternoon blowing soap bubbles
And it is with a feeling of delight I realize I am
All alone in the skittish darkness.
The birch-pods come clattering down on the weed-grown marble
    pavement.
And a curl of smoke stands above the triangular wooden roof.

Seventeen years in the capital of Foo-Yung province!
Surely woman was born for something
Besides continual fornication, retarded only by menstrual cramps.

I had thought of announcing my engagement to you
On the day of the first full moon of X month.

The wind has stopped, but the magnolia blossoms still
Fall with a plop onto the dry, spongy earth.
The evening air is pestiferous with midges.

There is only one way of completing the puzzle:
By finding a hog-shaped piece that is light green shading to buff at one
    side.

It is the beginning of March, a few
Russet and yellow wallflowers are blooming in the border
Protected by moss-grown, fragmentary masonry.

One morning you appear at breakfast
Dressed, as for a journey, in your worst suit of clothes.
And over a pot of coffee, or, more accurately, rusted water
Announce your intention of leaving me alone in this cistern-like house.
In your own best interests I shall decide not to believe you.

I think there is a funny sand bar
Beyond the old boardwalk
Your intrigue makes you understand.

"At thirty-two I came up to take my examination at the university.
The U wax factory, it seemed, wanted a new general manager.
I was the sole applicant for the job, but it was refused me.
So I have preferred to finish my life
In the quietude of this floral retreat."

The tiresome old man is telling us his life story.

Trout are circling under water—

Masters of eloquence
Glisten on the pages of your book
Like mountains veiled by water or the sky.

The "second position"
Comes in the seventeenth year
Watching the meaningless gyrations of flies above a sill.

Heads in hands, waterfall of simplicity.
The delta of living into everything.

The pump is busted. I shall have to get it fixed.

Your knotted hair
Around your shoulders
A shawl the color of the spectrum

Like that marvelous thing you haven't learned yet.

To refuse the square hive,
                              postpone the highest . . .

The apples are all getting tinted
In the cool light of autumn.

The constellations are rising
In perfect order: Taurus, Leo, Gemini.

From
THE
DOUBLE
DREAM
OF
SPRING

THE TASK

They are preparing to begin again:
Problems, new pennant up the flagpole
In a predicated romance.

About the time the sun begins to cut laterally across
The western hemisphere with its shadows, its carnival echoes,
The fugitive lands crowd under separate names.
It is the blankness that follows gaiety, and Everyman must depart
Out there into stranded night, for his destiny
Is to return unfruitful out of the lightness
That passing time evokes. It was only
Cloud-castles, adept to seize the past
And possess it, through hurting. And the way is clear
Now for linear acting into that time
In whose corrosive mass he first discovered how to breathe.

Just look at the filth you've made,
See what you've done.
Yet if these are regrets they stir only lightly
The children playing after supper,
Promise of the pillow and so much in the night to come.
I plan to stay here a little while
For these are moments only, moments of insight,
And there are reaches to be attained,
A last level of anxiety that melts
In becoming, like miles under the pilgrim's feet.

SPRING DAY

The immense hope, and forbearance
Trailing out of night, to sidewalks of the day
Like air breathed into a paper city, exhaled
As night returns bringing doubts

That swarm around the sleeper's head
But are fended off with clubs and knives, so that morning
Installs again in cold hope
The air that was yesterday, is what you are,

In so many phases the head slips from the hand.
The tears ride freely, laughs or sobs:
What do they matter? There is free giving and taking;
The giant body relaxed as though beside a stream

Wakens to the force of it and has to recognize
The secret sweetness before it turns into life—
Sucked out of many exchanges, torn from the womb,
Disinterred before completely dead—and heaves

Its mountain-broad chest. "They were long in coming,
Those others, and mattered so little that it slowed them
To almost nothing. They were presumed dead,
Their names honorably grafted on the landscape

To be a memory to men. Until today
We have been living in their shell.
Now we break forth like a river breaking through a dam,
Pausing over the puzzled, frightened plain,

And our further progress shall be terrible,
Turning fresh knives in the wounds
In that gulf of recreation, that bare canvas
As matter-of-fact as the traffic and the day's noise."

The mountain stopped shaking; its body
Arched into its own contradiction, its enjoyment,
As far from us lights were put out, memories of boys and girls
Who walked here before the great change,

Before the air mirrored us,
Taking the opposite shape of our effort,
Its inseparable comment and corollary
But casting us farther and farther out.

Wha—what happened? You are with
The orange tree, so that its summer produce
Can go back to where we got it wrong, then drip gently
Into history, if it wants to. A page turned; we were

Just now floundering in the wind of its colossal death.
And whether it is Thursday, or the day is stormy,
With thunder and rain, or the birds attack each other,
We have rolled into another dream.

No use charging the barriers of that other:
It no longer exists. But you,
Gracious and growing thing, with those leaves like stars,
We shall soon give all our attention to you.

PLAINNESS IN DIVERSITY

Silly girls your heads full of boys
There is a last sample of talk on the outer side
Your stand at last lifts to dumb evening.
It is reflected in the steep blue sides of the crater,
So much water shall wash over these our breaths
Yet shall remain unwashed at the end. The fine
Branches of the fir tree catch at it, ebbing.
Not on our planet is the destiny
That can make you one.

To be placed on the side of some mountain
Is the truer story, with the breath only
Coming in patches at first, and then the little spurt
The way a steam engine starts up eventually.
The sagas purposely ignore how better off it was next day,
The feeling in between the chapters, like fins.
There is so much they must say, and it is important
About all the swimming motions, and the way the hands
Came up out of the ocean with original fronds,
The famous arrow, the girls who came at dawn
To pay a visit to the young child, and how, when he grew up to be a man
The same restive ceremony replaced the limited years between,
Only now he was old, and forced to begin the journey to the sun.

SOONEST MENDED

Barely tolerated, living on the margin
In our technological society, we were always having to be rescued
On the brink of destruction, like heroines in *Orlando Furioso*
Before it was time to start all over again.
There would be thunder in the bushes, a rustling of coils,
And Angelica, in the Ingres painting, was considering
The colorful but small monster near her toe, as though wondering
  whether forgetting
The whole thing might not, in the end, be the only solution.
And then there always came a time when
Happy Hooligan in his rusted green automobile
Came plowing down the course, just to make sure everything was O.K.,
Only by that time we were in another chapter and confused
About how to receive this latest piece of information.
Was it information? Weren't we rather acting this out
For someone else's benefit, thoughts in a mind
With room enough and to spare for our little problems (so they began to
  seem),
Our daily quandary about food and the rent and bills to be paid?
To reduce all this to a small variant,
To step free at last, minuscule on the gigantic plateau—
This was our ambition: to be small and clear and free.
Alas, the summer's energy wanes quickly,
A moment and it is gone. And no longer
May we make the necessary arrangements, simple as they are.
Our star was brighter perhaps when it had water in it.
Now there is no question even of that, but only
Of holding on to the hard earth so as not to get thrown off,
With an occasional dream, a vision: a robin flies across
The upper corner of the window, you brush your hair away
And cannot quite see, or a wound will flash
Against the sweet faces of the others, something like:
This is what you wanted to hear, so why
Did you think of listening to something else? We are all talkers

It is true, but underneath the talk lies
The moving and not wanting to be moved, the loose
Meaning, untidy and simple like a threshing floor.

These then were some hazards of the course,
Yet though we knew the course *was* hazards and nothing else
It was still a shock when, almost a quarter of a century later,
The clarity of the rules dawned on you for the first time.
They were the players, and we who had struggled at the game
Were merely spectators, though subject to its vicissitudes
And moving with it out of the tearful stadium, borne on shoulders, at last.
Night after night this message returns, repeated
In the flickering bulbs of the sky, raised past us, taken away from us,
Yet ours over and over until the end that is past truth,
The being of our sentences, in the climate that fostered them,
Not ours to own, like a book, but to be with, and sometimes
To be without, alone and desperate.
But the fantasy makes it ours, a kind of fence-sitting
Raised to the level of an esthetic ideal. These were moments, years,
Solid with reality, faces, namable events, kisses, heroic acts,
But like the friendly beginning of a geometrical progression
Not too reassuring, as though meaning could be cast aside some day
When it had been outgrown. Better, you said, to stay cowering
Like this in the early lessons, since the promise of learning
Is a delusion, and I agreed, adding that
Tomorrow would alter the sense of what had already been learned,
That the learning process is extended in this way, so that from this
    standpoint
None of us ever graduates from college,
For time is an emulsion, and probably thinking not to grow up
Is the brightest kind of maturity for us, right now at any rate.
And you see, both of us were right, though nothing
Has somehow come to nothing; the avatars
Of our conforming to the rules and living

Around the home have made—well, in a sense, "good citizens" of us,
Brushing the teeth and all that, and learning to accept
The charity of the hard moments as they are doled out,
For this is action, this not being sure, this careless
Preparing, sowing the seeds crooked in the furrow,
Making ready to forget, and always coming back
To the mooring of starting out, that day so long ago.

SUMMER

There is that sound like the wind
Forgetting in the branches that means something
Nobody can translate. And there is the sobering "later on,"
When you consider what a thing meant, and put it down.

For the time being the shadow is ample
And hardly seen, divided among the twigs of a tree,
The trees of a forest, just as life is divided up
Between you and me, and among all the others out there.

And the thinning-out phase follows
The period of reflection. And suddenly, to be dying
Is not a little or mean or cheap thing,
Only wearying, the heat unbearable,

And also the little mindless constructions put upon
Our fantasies of what we did: summer, the ball of pine needles,
The loose fates serving our acts, with token smiles,
Carrying out their instructions too accurately—

Too late to cancel them now—and winter, the twitter
Of cold stars at the pane, that describes with broad gestures
This state of being that is not so big after all.
Summer involves going down as a steep flight of steps

To a narrow ledge over the water. Is this it, then,
This iron comfort, these reasonable taboos,
Or did you mean it when you stopped? And the face
Resembles yours, the one reflected in the water.

IT WAS RAINING IN THE CAPITAL

It was raining in the capital
And for many days and nights
The one they called the Aquarian
Had stayed alone with her delight.

What with the winter and its business
It had fallen to one side
And she had only recently picked it up
Where the other had died.

Between the pages of the newspaper
It smiled like a face.
Next to the drugstore on the corner
It looked to another place.

Or it would just hang around
Like sullen clouds over the sun.
But—this was the point—it was real
To her and to everyone.

For spring had entered the capital
Walking on gigantic feet.
The smell of witch hazel indoors
Changed to narcissus in the street.

She thought she had seen all this before:
Bundles of new, fresh flowers,
All changing, pressing upward
To the distant office towers.

Until now nothing had been easy,
Hemmed in by all that shit—
Horseshit, dogshit, birdshit, manshit—
Yes, she remembered having said it,

Having spoken in that way, thinking
There could be no road ahead,
Sobbing into the intractable presence of it
As one weeps alone in bed.

Its chamber was narrower than a seed
Yet when the doorbell rang
It reduced all that living to air
As *"kyrie eleison"* it sang.

Hearing that music he had once known
But now forgotten, the man,
The one who had waited casually in the dark
Turned to smile at the door's span.

He smiled and shrugged—a lesson
In the newspaper no longer
But fed by the ink and paper
Into a sign of something stronger

Who reads the news and takes the bus
Going to work each day
But who was never born of woman
Nor formed of the earth's clay.

Then what unholy bridegroom
Did the Aquarian foretell?
Or was such lively intelligence
Only the breath of hell?

It scarcely mattered at the moment
And it shall never matter at all
Since the moment will not be replaced
But stand, poised for its fall,

Forever. "This is what my learning
Teaches," the Aquarian said,
"To absorb life through the pores
For the life around you is dead."

The sun came out in the capital
Just before it set.
The lovely death's head shone in the sky
As though these two had never met.

VARIATIONS, CALYPSO AND FUGUE
ON A THEME OF ELLA WHEELER WILCOX

"For the pleasures of the many
May be ofttimes traced to one
As the hand that plants an acorn
Shelters armies from the sun."
And in places where the annual rainfall is .0071 inches
What a pleasure to lie under the tree, to sit, stand, and get up under
   the tree!
Im wunderschönen Monat Mai
The feeling is of never wanting to leave the tree,
Of predominantly peace and relaxation.
Do you step out from under the shade a moment,
It is only to return with renewed expectation, of expectation fulfilled.
Insecurity be damned! There is something to all this, that will not elude
   us:
Growing up under the shade of friendly trees, with our brothers all
   around.
And truly, young adulthood was never like this:
Such delight, such consideration, such affirmation in the way the day goes
   round together.
Yes, the world goes round a good deal faster
When there are highlights on the lips, unspoken and true words in the
   heart,
And the hand keeps brushing away a strand of chestnut hair, only to have
   it fall back into place again.
But all good things must come to an end, and so one must move forward
Into the space left by one's conclusions. Is this growing old?
Well, it is a good experience, to divest oneself of some tested ideals, some
   old standbys,
And even finding nothing to put in their place is a good experience,
Preparing one, as it does, for the consternation that is to come.
But—and this is the gist of it—what if I dreamed it all,
The branches, the late afternoon sun,

The trusting camaraderie, the love that watered all,
Disappearing promptly down into the roots as it should?
For later in the vast gloom of cities, only there you learn
How the ideas were good only because they had to die,
Leaving you alone and skinless, a drawing by Vesalius.
This is what was meant, and toward which everything directs:
That the tree should shrivel in 120-degree heat, the acorns
Lie around on the worn earth like eyeballs, and the lead soldiers shrug and
    slink off.

So my youth was spent, underneath the trees
I always moved around with perfect ease

I voyaged to Paris at the age of ten
And met many prominent literary men

Gazing at the Alps was quite a sight
I felt the tears flow forth with all their might

A climb to the Acropolis meant a lot to me
I had read the Greek philosophers you see

In the Colosseum I thought my heart would burst
Thinking of all the victims who had been there first

On Mount Ararat's side I began to grow
Remembering the Flood there, so long ago

On the banks of the Ganges I stood in mud
And watched the water light up like blood

The Great Wall of China is really a thrill
It cleaves through the air like a silver pill

It was built by the hand of man for good or ill
Showing what he can do when he decides not to kill

But of all the sights that were seen by me
In the East or West, on land or sea,
The best was the place that is spelled H-O-M-E.

Now that once again I have achieved home
I shall forbear all further urge to roam

There is a hole of truth in the green earth's rug
Once you find it you are as snug as a bug

Maybe some do not like it quite as much as you
That isn't all you're going to do.

You must remember that it is yours
Which is why nobody is sending you flowers

This age-old truth I to thee impart
Act according to the dictates of your art

Because if you don't no one else is going to
And that person isn't likely to be you.

It is the wind that comes from afar
It is the truth of the farthest star

In all likelihood you will not need these
So take it easy and learn your ABC's

And trust in the dream that will never come true
'Cause that is the scheme that is best for you
And the gleam that is the most suitable too.

"MAKE MY DREAM COME TRUE." This message, set in 84-point Hobo type, startled in the morning editions of the paper: the old, half-won security troubles the new pause. And with the approach of the holidays, the present is clearly here to stay: the big brass band of its particular moment's consciousness invades the plazas and the narrow alleys. Three-fourths of the houses in this city are on narrow stilts, finer than a girl's wrists: it is largely a question of keeping one's feet dry, and of privacy. In the morning you forget what the punishment was. Probably it was something like eating a pretzel or going into the back yard. Still, you can't tell. These things could be a lot clearer without hurting anybody. But it does not follow that such issues will produce the most dynamic capital gains for you.

Friday. We are really missing you.

"The most suitable," however, was not the one specially asked for nor the one hanging around the lobby. It was just the one asked after, day after day—what spilled over, claimed by the spillway. The distinction of a dog, of how a dog walks. The thought of a dog walking. No one ever referred to the incident again. The case was officially closed. Maybe there were choruses of silent gratitude, welling up in the spring night like a column of cloud, reaching to the very rafters of the sky—but this was their own business. The point is no ear ever heard them. Thus, the incident, to call it by one of its names—choice, conduct, absent-minded frown might be others—came to be not only as though it had never happened, but as though it never *could* have happened. Sealed into the wall of all that season's coming on. And thus, for a mere handful of people—roustabouts and degenerates, most of them—it became the only true version. Nothing else mattered. It was bread by morning and night, the dates falling listlessly from the trees—man, woman, child, festering glistering in a single orb. The reply to "hello."

> Pink purple and blue
> The way you used to do

The next two days passed oddly for Peter and Christine, and were among the most absorbing they had ever known. On the one hand, a vast open basin—or sea; on the other a narrow spit of land, terminating in a copse, with a few broken-down outbuildings lying here and there. It made no difference that the bey—b-e-y this time, oriental potentate—had ordained their release, there was this funny feeling that they should always be there, sustained by looks out over the ether, missing Mother and Alan and the others but really quiet, in a kind of activity that offers its own way of life, sunflower chained to the sun. Can it ever be resolved? Or are the forms of a person's thoughts controlled by inexorable laws, as in Dürer's Adam and Eve? So mutually exclusive, and so steep—Himalayas jammed side by side like New York apartment buildings. Oh the blame of it, the de-crescendo. My vice is worry. Forget it. The continual splitting up, the ear-shattering volumes of a polar ice-cap breaking up are just what you wanted. You've got it, so shut up.

> The crystal haze
> For days and days

Lots of sleep is an important factor, and rubbing the eyes. Getting off the subway he suddenly felt hungry. He went into one place, a place he knew, and ordered a hamburger and a cup of coffee. He hadn't been in this neighborhood in a long time—not since he was a kid. He used to play stickball in the vacant lot across the street. Sometimes his bunch would get into a fight with some of the older boys, and he'd go home tired and bleeding. Most days were the same though. He'd say "Hi" to the other kids and they'd say "Hi" to him. Nice bunch of guys. Finally he decided to take a turn past the old grade school he'd attended as a kid. It was a rambling structure of yellow brick, now gone in seediness and shabbiness which the late-afternoon shadows mercifully softened. The gravel playground in front was choked with weeds. Large trees and shrubbery would do no harm flanking the main entrance. Time farted.

The first shock rattles the cruets in their stand,
The second rips the door from its hinges.

"My dear friend," he said gently, "you said you were Professor Hertz. You must pardon me if I say that the information startles and mystifies me. When you are stronger I have some questions to ask you, if you will be kind enough to answer them."

No one was prepared for the man's answer to that apparently harmless statement.

Weak as he was, Gustavus Hertz raised himself on his elbow. He stared wildly about him, peering fearfully into the shadowy corners of the room.

"I will tell you nothing! Nothing, do you hear?" he shrieked. "Go away! Go away!"

SONG

The song tells us of our old way of living,
Of life in former times. Fragrance of florals,
How things merely ended when they ended,
Of beginning again into a sigh. Later

Some movement is reversed and the urgent masks
Speed toward a totally unexpected end
Like clocks out of control. Is this the gesture
That was meant, long ago, the curving in

Of frustrated denials, like jungle foliage
And the simplicity of the ending all to be let go
In quick, suffocating sweetness? The day
Puts toward a nothingness of sky

Its face of rusticated brick. Sooner or later,
The cars lament, the whole business will be hurled down.
Meanwhile we sit, scarcely daring to speak,
To breathe, as though this closeness cost us life.

The pretensions of a past will some day
Make it over into progress, a growing up,
As beautiful as a new history book
With uncut pages, unseen illustrations,

And the purpose of the many stops and starts will be made clear:
Backing into the old affair of not wanting to grow
Into the night, which becomes a house, a parting of the ways
Taking us far into sleep. A dumb love.

DECOY

We hold these truths to be self-evident:
That ostracism, both political and moral, has
Its place in the twentieth-century scheme of things;
That urban chaos is the problem we have been seeing into and seeing into,
For the factory, deadpanned by its very existence into a
Descending code of values, has moved right across the road from total
    financial upheaval
And caught regression head-on. The descending scale does not imply
A corresponding deterioration of moral values, punctuated
By acts of corporate vandalism every five years,
Like a bunch of violets pinned to a dress, that knows and ignores its own
    standing.
There is every reason to rejoice with those self-styled prophets of commer-
    cial disaster, those harbingers of gloom,
Over the imminent lateness of the denouement that, advancing slowly,
    never arrives,
At the same time keeping the door open to a tongue-in-cheek attitude on
    the part of the perpetrators,
The men who sit down to their vast desks on Monday to begin planning
    the week's notations, jotting memoranda that take
Invisible form in the air, like flocks of sparrows
Above the city pavements, turning and wheeling aimlessly
But on the average directed by discernible motives.

To sum up: We are fond of plotting itineraries
And our pyramiding memories, alert as dandelion fuzz, dart from one
    pretext to the next
Seeking in occasions new sources of memories, for memory is profit
Until the day it spreads out all its accumulation, delta-like, on the plain
For that day no good can come of remembering, and the anomalies cancel
    each other out.
But until then foreshortened memories will keep us going, alive, one to the
    other.

There was never any excuse for this and perhaps there need be none,
For kicking out into the morning, on the wide bed,
Waking far apart on the bed, the two of them:
Husband and wife
Man and wife

FOR JOHN CLARE

Kind of empty in the way it sees everything, the earth gets to its feet and salutes the sky. More of a success at it this time than most others it is. The feeling that the sky might be in the back of someone's mind. Then there is no telling how many there are. They grace everything—bush and tree—to take the roisterer's mind off his caroling—so it's like a smooth switch back. To what was aired in their previous conniption fit. There is so much to be seen everywhere that it's like not getting used to it, only there is so much it never feels new, never any different. You are standing looking at that building and you cannot take it all in, certain details are already hazy and the mind boggles. What will it all be like in five years' time when you try to remember? Will there have been boards in between the grass part and the edge of the street? As long as that couple is stopping to look in that window over there we cannot go. We feel like they have to tell us we can, but they never look our way and they are already gone, gone far into the future—the night of time. If we could look at a photograph of it and say there they are, they never really stopped but there they are. There is so much to be said, and on the surface of it very little gets said.

There ought to be room for more things, for a spreading out, like. Being immersed in the details of rock and field and slope—letting them come to you for once, and then meeting them halfway would be so much easier—if they took an ingenuous pride in being in one's blood. Alas, we perceive them if at all as those things that were meant to be put aside—costumes of the supporting actors or voice trilling at the end of a narrow enclosed street. You can do nothing with them. Not even offer to pay.

It is possible that finally, like coming to the end of a long, barely perceptible rise, there is mutual cohesion and interaction. The whole scene is fixed in your mind, the music all present, as though you could see each note as well as hear it. I say this because there is an uneasiness in things just now. Waiting for something to be over before you are forced to notice it. The pollarded trees scarcely bucking the wind—and yet it's keen, it makes you fall over. Clabbered sky. Seasons that pass with a rush. After all it's their time too—nothing says they aren't to make something of it. As for Jenny Wren, she cares, hopping about on her little twig like she was tryin' to tell us somethin', but that's just it, she couldn't even if she wanted to—

dumb bird. But the others—and they in some way must know too—it would never occur to them to want to, even if they could take the first step of the terrible journey toward feeling somebody should act, that ends in utter confusion and hopelessness, east of the sun and west of the moon. So their comment is: "No comment." Meanwhile the whole history of probabilities is coming to life, starting in the upper left-hand corner, like a sail.

FARM IMPLEMENTS AND RUTABAGAS
IN A LANDSCAPE

The first of the undecoded messages read: "Popeye sits in thunder,
Unthought of. From that shoebox of an apartment,
From livid curtain's hue, a tangram emerges: a country."
Meanwhile the Sea Hag was relaxing on a green couch: "How pleasant
To spend one's vacation *en la casa de Popeye*," she scratched
Her cleft chin's solitary hair. She remembered spinach

And was going to ask Wimpy if he had bought any spinach.
"M'love," he intercepted, "the plains are decked out in thunder
Today, and it shall be as you wish." He scratched
The part of his head under his hat. The apartment
Seemed to grow smaller. "But what if no pleasant
Inspiration plunge us now to the stars? *For this is my country*."

Suddenly they remembered how it was cheaper in the country.
Wimpy was thoughtfully cutting open a number 2 can of spinach
When the door opened and Swee'pea crept in. "How pleasant!"
But Swee'pea looked morose. A note was pinned to his bib. "Thunder
And tears are unavailing," it read. "Henceforth shall Popeye's apartment
Be but remembered space, toxic or salubrious, whole or scratched."

Olive came hurtling through the window; its geraniums scratched
Her long thigh. "I have news!" she gasped. "Popeye, forced as you
    know to flee the country
One musty gusty evening, by the schemes of his wizened, duplicate
    father, jealous of the apartment
And all that it contains, myself and spinach
In particular, heaves bolts of loving thunder
At his own astonished becoming, rupturing the pleasant

Arpeggio of our years. No more shall pleasant
Rays of the sun refresh your sense of growing old, nor the scratched
Tree-trunks and mossy foliage, only immaculate darkness and
    thunder."

She grabbed Swee'pea. "I'm taking the brat to the country."
"But you can't do that—he hasn't even finished his spinach,"
Urged the Sea Hag, looking fearfully around at the apartment.

But Olive was already out of earshot. Now the apartment
Succumbed to a strange new hush. "Actually it's quite pleasant
Here," thought the Sea Hag. "If this is all we need fear from spinach
Then I don't mind so much. Perhaps we could invite Alice the Goon
    over"—she scratched
One dug pensively—"but Wimpy is such a country
Bumpkin, always burping like that." Minute at first, the thunder

Soon filled the apartment. It was domestic thunder,
The color of spinach. Popeye chuckled and scratched
His balls: it sure was pleasant to spend a day in the country.

PARERGON

We are happy in our way of life.
It doesn't make much sense to others. We sit about,
Read, and are restless. Occasionally it becomes time
To lower the dark shade over it all.
Our entity pivots on a self-induced trance
Like sleep. Noiseless our living stops
And one strays as in a dream
Into those respectable purlieus where life is motionless and alive
To utter the few words one knows:

"O woebegone people! Why so much crying,
Such desolation in the streets?
Is it the present of flesh, that each of you
At your jagged casement window should handle,
Nervous unto thirst and ultimate death?
Meanwhile the true way is sleeping;
Your lawful acts drink an unhealthy repose
From the upturned lip of this vessel, secretly,
But it is always time for a change.
That certain sins of omission go unpunished
Does not weaken your position
But this underbrush in which you are secure
Is its doing. Farewell then,
Until, under a better sky
We may meet expended, for just doing it
Is only an excuse. We need the tether
Of entering each other's lives, eyes wide apart, crying."

As one who moves forward from a dream
The stranger left that house on hastening feet
Leaving behind the woman with the face shaped like an arrowhead,
And all who gazed upon him wondered at
The strange activity around him.
How fast the faces kindled as he passed!

It was a marvel that no one spoke
To stem the river of his passing
Now grown to flood proportions, as on the sunlit mall
Or in the enclosure of some court
He took his pleasure, savage
And mild with the contemplating.
Yet each knew he saw only aspects,
That the continuity was fierce beyond all dream of enduring,
And turned his head away, and so
The lesson eddied far into the night:
Joyful its beams, and in the blackness blacker still,
Though undying joyousness, caught in that trap.

SOME WORDS

from the French of Arthur Cravan

Life is not at all what you might think it to be
A simple tale where each thing has its history
    It's much more than its scuffle and anything goes
Both evil and good, subject to the same laws.
    Each hour has its color and forever gives place
Leaving less than yon bird of itself a trace.
In vain does memory attempt to store away
The scent of its colors in a single bouquet
Memory can but shift cold ashes around
When the depths of time it endeavors to sound.
    Never think that you may be allowed, at the end,
To say to yourself, "I am of myself the friend,"
Or make with yourself a last reconciliation.
You will remain the victim of your hesitation
You will forget today before tomorrow is here
And disavow yourself while much is still far from clear.
    The defunct days will offer you their images
Only so that you may read of former outrages
And the days to come will mar with their complaints
The splendor that in your honor dejected evening paints.
    Wishing to collect in your heart the feelings
Scattered in the meadows of misfortune's hard dealings
You will be the shepherd whose dog has run away
You will know even less whence comes your dismay
Than you know the hour your boredom first saw the light.
    Weary of seeking day you will relish the night
In night's dim orchards you will find some rest
The counsels of the trees of night are best
Better than those of the tree of knowledge, which corrupts us at birth
And which you allowed to flourish in the accursèd earth.
    When your most arduous labors grow pale as death
And you begin to inhale autumn's chilly breath
Winter will come soon to batter with his mace
Your precious moments, scattering them all over the place.

You will always be having to get up from your chairs
To move on to other heartbreaks, be caught in other snares.
The seasons will revolve on their scented course
Solar or devastated you will perforce
Be perfumed at their tepid passing, and not know
Whether their fragrance brings you joy or woe.
At the moment when your life becomes a total shambles
You will have to resume your hopeless rambles
You have left everything behind and you still are eligible
And all alone, as the gulf becomes unbridgeable
You will have to earn your daily bread
Although you feel you'd be better off dead.
They'll hurt you, and you'd like to put up some resistance
Because you know that your very existence
Depends on others as unworthy of you
As you are of God, and when it's time to review
Your wrongs, you will feel no pain, they will seem a joke
For you will have ceased to suffer under their yoke.
Whether you pass through fields, towns or across the sea
You will always retain your melancholy
And look after it; you will have to think of your career
Not live it, as in a game where the best player
Is he who forgets himself, and cannot say
What spurs him on, and makes him win the day.
When weary henceforth of wishing to gaze
At the sinuous path of your spread-out days
You return to the place where your stables used to tower
You will find nothing left but some fetid manure
Your steeds beneath other horsemen will have fled
To autumn's far country, all rusted and red.
Like an ardent rose in the September sun
You will feel the flesh sag from your limbs, one by one,
Less of you than of a pruned rosebush will remain,
That spring lies in wait for, to clothe once again.

If you wish to love you won't know whom to choose
There are none whose love you'd be sorry to lose
Not to love at all would be the better part
Lest another seize and confiscate your heart.

When evening descends on your deserted routes
You won't be afraid and will say, "What boots
It to worry and fret? To rail at my luck?
Since time my actions like an apple will pluck."

You would like of yourself to curtail certain features
That you dislike, making allowances for this creature,
Giving that other one a chance to show his fettle,
Confining yet another behind bars of metal:
That rebel will soon become an armèd titan.

Then let yourself love all that you take delight in
Accept yourself whole, accept the heritage
That shaped you and is passed on from age to age
Down to your entity. Remain mysterious;
Rather than be pure, accept yourself as numerous.
The wave of heredity will not be denied:
Best, then, on a lover's silken breast to abide
And be wafted by her to Nirvana's blue shoals
Where the self is abolished and renounces its goals.

In you all things must live and procreate
Forget about the harvest and its sheaves of wheat
You are the harvest and not the reaper
And of your domain another is the keeper.

When you see the lapsed dreams that childhood invents
Salute your adolescence and fold their tents
Virginal, tall and slim beside the jasmine tree
An adorable girl is plaiting tenderly
The bouquet of love, which will stick in your memory
As the final vision and the final story.

Henceforth you will burn with lascivious fire

Accursèd passion will strum its lyre
At the charming crossroads where day is on the wane
As the curve of a hill dissolves in a plain.
        The tacit beauty of the sacred plateau
Will be spoiled for you and you will never know
Henceforth the peace a pious heart bestows
To the soul its gentle sister in whom it echoes;
Anxiety will have called everything into question
And you will be tempted to the wildest actions.
        Then let all fade at the edge of our days!
No God emerges to dream our destinies.
The days depart, only boredom does not retreat
It's like a path that flies beneath one's feet
Whose horizon shifts while as we trudge
The dust and mud stick to us and do not budge.
        In vain do we speak, provoke actions or think,
We are prisoners of the world's demented sink.
        The soft enchantments of our years of innocence
Are harvested by accredited experience
Our fondest memories soon turn to poison
And only oblivion remains in season.
        When, beside a window, one feels evening prevail
Who is there who can receive its slanting veil
And not regret day that bore it on its stream
Whether day was joy or under evil's regime
Drawing us to the one and deploring the other
Regretting the departure of all our brothers
And all that made the day, including its stains.
        Whoever you may be O man who complains
Not at your destiny, can you then doubt,
When the moment arrives for you to stretch out,
That remorse, a stinking jackal with subtle nose,
Will come at the end to devour your repose?
        . . . Something gentle and something sad eftsoons

In the flanks of our pale and realistic noons
Holds with our soul a discourse without end
The curtain rises on the afternoon wind
Day sheds its leaves and now will soon be gone
And already my adulthood seems to mourn
Beside the reddish sunsets of the hollow vase
As gently it starts to deepen and slowly to increase.

THE BUNGALOWS

Impatient as we were for all of them to join us,
The land had not yet risen into view: gulls had swept the gray steel
    towers away
So that it profited less to go searching, away over the humming earth
Than to stay in immediate relation to these other things—boxes, store
    parts, whatever you wanted to call them—
Whose installedness was the price of further revolutions, so you knew
    this combat was the last.
And still the relationship waxed, billowed like scenery on the breeze.

They are the same aren't they,
The presumed landscape and the dream of home
Because the people are all homesick today or desperately sleeping,
Trying to remember how those rectangular shapes
Became so extraneous and so near
To create a foreground of quiet knowledge
In which youth had grown old, chanting and singing wise hymns that
Will sign for old age
And so lift up the past to be persuaded, and be put down again.

The warning is nothing more than an aspirate "h";
The problem is sketched completely, like fireworks mounted on poles:
Complexion of evening, the accurate voices of the others.
During Coca-Cola lessons it becomes patent
Of noise on the left, and we had so skipped a stage that
The great wave of the past, compounded in derision,
Submerged idea and non-dreamer alike
In falsetto starlight like "purity"
Of design that had been the first danger sign
To wash the sticky, icky stuff down the drain—pfui!

How does it feel to be outside and inside at the same time,
The delicious feeling of the air contradicting and secretly abetting

The interior warmth? But land curdles the dismay in which it's written
Bearing to a final point of folly and doom
The wisdom of these generations.
Look at what you've done to the landscape—
The ice cube, the olive—
There is a perfect tri-city mesh of things
Extending all the way along the river on both sides
With the end left for thoughts on construction
That are always turning to alps and thresholds
Above the tide of others, feeding a European moss rose without glory.

We shall very soon have the pleasure of recording
A period of unanimous tergiversation in this respect
And to make that pleasure the greater, it is worth while
At the risk of tedious iteration, to put first upon record a final protest:
Rather decaying art, genius, inspiration to hold to
An impossible "calque" of reality, than
"The new school of the trivial, rising up on the field of battle,
A thing of sludge and leaf-mold," and life
Goes trickling out through the holes, like water through a sieve,
All in one direction.

You who were directionless, and thought it would solve everything if
    you found one,
What do you make of this? Just because a thing is immortal
Is that any reason to worship it? Death, after all, is immortal.
But you have gone into your houses and shut the doors, meaning
There can be no further discussion.
And the river pursues its lonely course
With the sky and the trees cast up from the landscape
For green brings unhappiness—*le vert porte malheur.*
"The chartreuse mountain on the absinthe plain
Makes the strong man's tears tumble down like rain."

All this came to pass eons ago.
Your program worked out perfectly. You even avoided
The monotony of perfection by leaving in certain flaws:
A backward way of becoming, a forced handshake,
An absent-minded smile, though in fact nothing was left to chance.
Each detail was startlingly clear, as though seen through a magnifying
  glass,
Or would have been to an ideal observer, namely yourself—
For only you could watch yourself so patiently from afar
The way God watches a sinner on the path to redemption,
Sometimes disappearing into valleys, but always *on the way*,
For it all builds up into something, meaningless or meaningful
As architecture, because planned and then abandoned when completed,
To live afterwards, in sunlight and shadow, a certain amount of years.
Who cares about what was there before? There is no going back,
For standing still means death, and life is moving on,
Moving on towards death. But sometimes standing still is also life.

THE CHATEAU HARDWARE

It was always November there. The farms
Were a kind of precinct; a certain control
Had been exercised. The little birds
Used to collect along the fence.
It was the great "as though," the how the day went,
The excursions of the police
As I pursued my bodily functions, wanting
Neither fire nor water,
Vibrating to the distant pinch
And turning out the way I am, turning out to greet you.

SORTES VERGILIANAE

You have been living now for a long time and there is nothing you do not
    know.
Perhaps something you read in the newspaper influenced you and that was
    very frequently.
They have left you to think along these lines and you have gone your own
    way because you guessed that
Under their hiding was the secret, casual as breath, betrayed for the asking.
Then the sky opened up, revealing much more than any of you were
    intended to know.
It is a strange thing how fast the growth is, almost as fast as the light from
    polar regions
Reflected off the arctic ice-cap in summer. When you know where it is
    heading
You have to follow it, though at a sadly reduced rate of speed,
Hence folly and idleness, raging at the confines of some miserable sunlit
    alley or court.
It is the nature of these people to embrace each other, they know no other
    kind but themselves.
Things pass quickly out of sight and the best is to be forgotten quickly
For it is wretchedness that endures, shedding its cancerous light on all it
    approaches:
Words spoken in the heat of passion, that might have been retracted in good
    time,
All good intentions, all that was arguable. These are stilled now, as the
    embrace in the hollow of its flux
And can never be revived except as perverse notations on an indisputable
    state of things,
As conduct in the past, vanished from the reckoning long before it was
    time.
Lately you've found the dull fevers still inflict their round, only they are
    unassimilable
Now that newness or importance has worn away. It is with us like day and
    night,

The surge upward through the grade-school positioning and bursting into
   soft gray blooms
Like vacuum-cleaner sweepings, the opulent fuzz of our cage, or like an
   excited insect
In nervous scrimmage for the head, etching its none-too-complex ordi-
   nances into the matter of the day.
Presently all will go off satisfied, leaving the millpond bare, a site for new
   picnics,
As they came, naked, to explore all the possible grounds on which ex-
   changes could be set up.
It is "No Fishing" in modest capital letters, and getting out from under the
   major weight of the thing
As it was being indoctrinated and dropped, heavy as a branch with apples,
And as it started to sigh, just before tumbling into your lap, chagrined and
   satisfied at the same time,
Knowing its day over and your patience only beginning, toward what
   marvels of speculation, auscultation, world-view,
Satisfied with the entourage. It is this blank carcass of whims and tentative
   afterthoughts
Which is being delivered into your hand like a letter some forty-odd years
   after the day it was posted.
Strange, isn't it, that the message makes some sense, if only a relative one
   in the larger context of message-receiving
That you will be called to account for just as the purpose of it is becoming
   plain,
Being one and the same with the day it set out, though you cannot imagine
   this.
There was a time when the words dug in, and you laughed and joked,
   accomplice
Of all the possibilities of their journey through the night and the stars,
   creature
Who looked to the abandonment of such archaic forms as these, and mean-
   while

Supported them as the tools that made you. The rut became apparent only later

And by then it was too late to check such expansive aspects as what to do while waiting

For the others to show: unfortunately no pile of tattered magazines was in evidence,

Such dramas sleeping below the surface of the everyday machinery; besides

Quality is not given to everybody, and who are you to have been supposing you had it?

So the journey grew ever slower; the battlements of the city could now be discerned from afar

But meanwhile the water was giving out and malaria had decimated their ranks and undermined their morale,

You know the story, so that if turning back was unthinkable, so was victorious conquest of the great brazen gates.

Best perhaps to fold up right here, but even that was not to be granted.

Some days later in the pulsating of orchestras someone asked for a drink:

The music stopped and those who had been confidently counting the rhythms grew pale.

This is just a footnote, though a microcosmic one perhaps, to the greater curve

Of the elaboration; it asks no place in it, only insertion *hors-texte* as the invisible notion of how that day grew

From planisphere to heaven, and what part in it all the "I" had, the insatiable researcher of learned trivia, bookworm,

And one who marched along with, "made common cause," yet had neither the gumption nor the desire to trick the thing into happening,

Only long patience, as the star climbs and sinks, leaving illumination to the setting sun.

From
*THREE
POEMS*

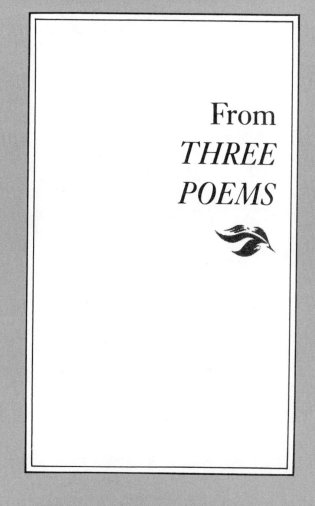

THE SYSTEM

The system was breaking down. The one who had wandered alone past so many happenings and events began to feel, backing up along the primal vein that led to his center, the beginning of a hiccup that would, if left to gather, explode the center to the extremities of life, the suburbs through which one makes one's way to where the country is.

At this time of life whatever being there is is doing a lot of listening, as though to the feeling of the wind before it starts, and it slides down this anticipation of itself, already full-fledged, a lightning existence that has come into our own. The trees and the streets are there merely to divide it up, to prevent it from getting all over itself, from retreating into itself instead of logically unshuffling into this morning that had to be, of the day of temptation. It is with some playfulness that we actually sit down to the business of mastering the many pauses and the abrupt, sharp accretions of regular being in the clotted sphere of today's activities. As though this were just any old day. There is no need for setting out, to advertise one's destination. All the facts are here and it remains only to use them in the right combinations, but that building will be the size of today, the rooms habitable and leading into one another in a lasting sequence, eternal and of the greatest timeliness.

It is all that. But there was time for others, that were to have got under way, sequences that now can exist only in memory, for there were other times for them. Yet they really existed. For instance a jagged kind of mood that comes at the end of the day, lifting life into the truth of real pain for a few moments before subsiding in the usual irregular way, as things do. These were as much there as anything, things to be fumbled with, cringed before: dry churrings of no timbre, hysterical staccato passages that one cannot master or turn away from. These things led into life. Now they are gone but it remains, calm, lucid, but weightless, drifting above everything and everybody like a light in the sky, no more to be surmised, only remembered as so many things that remain at equal distances from us are remembered. The light drinks the dark and sinks down, not on top of us as we had expected but far, far from us in some other, unrelated sphere. This was not even the life that was going to happen to us. It was different in those days, though. Men felt things differently and their reactions were different. It was all life, this truth, you forgot about it and it was there. No need to collect your thoughts at every moment before putting forth a hesitant feeler into the rank and file of their sensations: the truth was obstinately itself, so much so that it always seemed about to harden and shrink, to grow hard and dark and vanish into itself anxiously but stubbornly, but this was just the other side of the coin of its intense conviction. It really knew what it *was*. Meanwhile the life uncurled around it in calm waves, unimpressed by the severity and yet not paying much mind, also very much itself. It seemed as though innumerable transparent tissues hovered around these two entities and joined them in some way, and yet when one looked there was nothing special to be seen, only miles and miles of buoyancy, the way the mild blue sky of a summer afternoon seems to support a distant soaring bird. This was the outside reality. Inside there was like a bare room, or an alphabet, an alphabet of clemency. Now at last you knew what you were supposed to know. The words formed from it and the sentences formed from them were dry and clear, as though made of wood. There wasn't too much of any one thing. The feelings never wandered off into a private song or tried to present the procession of straightforward facts as something like a pageant: the gorgeous was still unknown. There was, however, a residue, a kind of fiction that developed parallel to the classic truths of daily life (as it was in that heroic but commonplace age) as they unfolded with the foreseeable majesty of a holocaust, an unfrightening one, and went unrecognized, drawing force and grandeur from this like the illegitimate offspring of a king. It is this "other tradition" which we propose to explore. The facts of history have been too well rehearsed (I'm speaking needless to say not of written history but the oral kind that goes on in you without your having to do anything about it) to require further elucidation here. But the other, unrelated happenings that form a kind of sequence of fantastic reflections as they succeed each other at a pace and according to an inner necessity of their own—these, I say, have hardly ever been looked at from a vantage point other than the historian's and an arcane historian's at that. The living aspect of these obscure phenomena has never to my knowledge been examined from a point of view like the painter's: in the round, bathed in a sufficient flow of overhead light, with "all its imperfections on its head" and yet without prejudice of the exaggerations either of the anathematist or the eulogist: quietly, in short, and I hope succinctly. Judged from this angle the whole affair will, I think, partake of and benefit from the enthusiasm not of the religious fanatic but of the average, open-minded, intelligent person who has never interested himself before in these matters either from not having had the leisure to do so or from ignorance of their existence.

From the outset it was apparent that someone had played a colossal trick on something. The switches had been tripped, as it were; the entire world or one's limited but accurate idea of it was bathed in glowing love, of a sort that need never have come into being but was now indispensable as air is to living creatures. It filled up the whole universe, raising the temperature of all things. Not an atom but did not feel obscurely compelled to set out in search of a mate; not a living creature, no insect or rodent, that didn't feel the obscure twitchings of dormant love, that didn't ache to join in the universal turmoil and hullabaloo that fell over the earth, roiling the clear waters of the reflective intellect, getting it into all kinds of messes that could have been avoided if only, as Pascal says, we had the sense to stay in our room, but the individual will condemns this notion and sallies forth full of ardor and *hubris*, bent on self-discovery in the guise of an attractive partner who is *the* heaven-sent one, the convex one with whom he has had the urge to mate all these seasons without realizing it. Thus a state of positively sinful disquiet began to prevail wherein men's eyes could be averted from the truth by the passing of a romantic stranger whose per-fume set in motion all kinds of idle and frivolous trains of thought leading who knows where—to hell, most likely, or at very best to a position of blankness and ill-conceived repose on the edge of the flood, so that looking down into it one no longer saw the comforting reflection of one's own face and felt secure in the knowledge that, whatever the outcome, the struggle was going on in the arena of one's own breast. The bases for true reflective thinking had been annihilated by the scourge, and at the same time there was the undeniable fact of exaltation on many fronts, of a sense of holiness growing up through the many kinds of passion like a tree with branches bearing candelabra higher and higher up until they almost vanish from sight and are confused with the stars whose earthly avatars they are: the celestial promise of delights to come in another world and still lovely to look at in this one. Thus, in a half-baked kind of way, this cosmic welter of attractions was coming to stand for the real thing, which has to be colorless and featureless if it is to be the true reflection of the primeval energy from which it issued forth, once a salient force capable of assuming the shape of any of the great impulses struggling to accomplish the universal task, but now bogged down in a single aspect of these to the detriment of the others, which begin to dwindle, jejeune, etiolated, as though not really essential, as though someone had devised them for the mere pleasure of complicating the already complicated texture of the byways and torments through which we have to stray, plagued by thorns, chased by wild beasts, as though it were not commonly known from the beginning that not one of these tendrils of the tree of humanity could be bruised without endangering the whole vast waving mass; that that gorgeous, motley organism would tumble or die out unless each particle of its well-being were conserved as preciously as the idea of the whole. For universal love is as special an aspect as carnal love or any of the other kinds: all forms of mental and spiritual activity must be practiced and encouraged equally if the whole affair is to prosper. There is no cutting corners where the life of the soul is concerned, even if a too modest approximation of the wish that caused it to begin to want to flower be the result—a result that could look like overpruning to the untrained eye. Thus it was that a kind of blight fell on these early forms of going forth and being together, an anarchy of the affections sprung from too much universal cohesion. Yet so blind are we to the true nature of reality at any given moment that this chaos—bathed, it is true, in the iridescent hues of the rainbow and clothed in an endless confusion of fair and variegated forms which did their best to stifle any burgeoning notions

hence a dilemma for any but the unrepentant hedonists or on the contrary those who chose to remain all day on the dung-heap, rending their hair and clothing and speaking of sackcloth and ashes: these, by far the noisiest group, made the least impression as usual, yet the very fact that they existed pointed to what seemed to be a tragic flaw in the system's structure; for among penance or perpetual feasting or the draconian requirements of a conscience eternally mobilized against itself, feeding on itself in order to re create itself in a shape that the next instant would destroy, how was one to choose? So that those who assumed that they had reached the end of an elaborate but basically simple progression, the logical last step of history, came more and more to be the dominant party: a motley group but with many level heads among them, whose voices chanting the wise maxims of regular power gradually approached the point of submerging the other cacophony of tinkling cymbals and wailing and individual voices raised in solemn but unreal debate. This was the logical cutting-off place, then: ahead might lie new forms of life, some of them beautiful perhaps, but the point was that the effort of establishing them or anything else that was to come had ended here: a permanent now had taken over and was free to recast the old forms, riddles that had been expected to last until the Day of Judgment, as it saw fit, in whatever shape seemed expedient for living the next few crucial moments into a future without controls.

It seemed, just for a moment, that a new point had now been reached. It was not the time for digressions yet it made them inevitable, like a curtain at the end of an act. It brought you to a pass where turning back was unthinkable, and where further progress was possible only after it had been discussed at length, but which also outlawed discussion. Life became a pregnant silence, but it was understood that the silence was to lead no-where. It became impossible to breathe easily in this constricted atmo-sphere. We ate little, for it seemed that in this way we could produce the inner emptiness from which alone understanding can spring up, the tree of contradictions, joyous and living, investing that hollow void with its com-plicated material self. At this time we were surrounded by old things, such as need not be questioned but which distill the meek information that is within them like a perfume on the air, to be used and disposed of; and also by certain new things which wear their newness like a quality, perhaps as an endorsement of the present, in all events as a vote of confidence in the currency of the just-created as a common language available to all men of good will, however disturbing the times themselves might turn out to be. Gradually one grew less aware of the idea of not turning back imposed as a condition for progress, as one imbibed the magic present that drew everything—the old and the new—along in the net of its infectious charm. Surely it would be possible to profit from the options of this cooperative new climate as though they were a charter instead of a vague sense of well-being, like a mild day in early spring, ready to be dashed to pieces by the first seasonable drop in temperature. And meanwhile there was a great sense of each one's going about his business, quiet in the elation of that accomplishment, as though it were enough to set one's foot on a certain path to be guaranteed of arriving at some destination. Yet the destinations were few. What actually was *wanted* from this constructive feeling? A "house by the side of the road" in which one could stay indefinitely, arranging new opportunities and fixing up old ones so that they mingled in a harmonious mass that could be called living with a sense of purpose? No, what was wanted and was precisely lacking in this gay and salubrious desert was an end to the "end" theory whereby each man was both an idol and the humblest of idolaters, in other words the antipodes of his own universe, his own redemption or his own damnation, with the rest of the world as a painted backdrop to his own monodrama of becoming of which he was the lone impassioned spectator. But the world avenges itself on those who would lose it by skipping over the due process of elimination, from whatever altruistic motive, by incrusting itself so thoroughly in these efforts at self-renewal that no amount of wriggling can dislodge its positive or negative image from all that is contemplated of present potentialities or the great sane simplifications to come. So that it was all lost, or rather all in the shade that instills weariness and sickness into the limbs under the guise of enraptured satiety. There was, again, no place to go, that is, no place that would not make a mockery of the place already left, casting all progress forward into the confusion of an eternally misapplied present. This was the stage to which reason and intuition working so well together had brought us, but it was scarcely their fault if now fear at the longest shadows of approaching darkness began to prompt thoughts of stopping somewhere for the night, as well as a serious doubt that any such place existed on the face of the earth.

On this Sunday which is also the last day of January let us pause for a moment to take note of where we are. A new year has just begun and now a new month is coming up, charged with its weight of promise and probable disappointments, standing in the wings like an actor who is conscious of nothing but the anticipated cue, totally absorbed, a pillar of waiting. And now there is no help for it but to be cast adrift in the new month. One is plucked from one month to the next; the year is like a fast-moving Ferris wheel; tomorrow all the riders will be under the sign of February and there is no appeal, one will have to get used to living with its qualities and perhaps one will even adjust to them successfully before the next month arrives with a whole string of new implications in its wake. Just to live this way is impossibly difficult, but the strange thing is that no one seems to notice it; people sail along quite comfortably and actually seem to enjoy the way the year progresses, and they manage to fill its widening space with multiple activities which apparently mean a lot to them. Of course some are sadder than the others but it doesn't seem to be because of the dictatorship of the months and years, and it goes away after a while. But the few who want order in their lives and a sense of growing and progression toward a fixed end suffer terribly. Sometimes they try to dope their consciousness of the shifting but ineluctable grid of time that has been arbitrarily imposed on them with alcohol or drugs, but these lead merely to mornings after whose waking is ten times more painful than before, bringing with it a new and more terrible realization of the impossibility of reconciling their own ends with those of the cosmos. If by chance you should be diverted or distracted for a moment from awareness of your imprisonment by some pleasant or interesting occurrence, there is always the shape of the individual day to remind you. It is a microcosm of man's life as it gently wanes, its long morning shadows getting shorter with the approach of noon, the high point of the day which could be likened to that sudden tremendous moment of intuition that comes only once in a lifetime, and then the fuller, more rounded shapes of early afternoon as the sun imperceptibly sinks in the sky and the shadows start to lengthen, until all are blotted in the stealthy coming of twilight, merciful in one sense that it hides the differences, blemishes as well as beauty marks, that gave the day its character and in so doing caused it to be another day in our limited span of days, the reminder that time is moving on and we are getting older, not older enough to make any difference on this particular occasion, but older all the same. Even now the sun is dropping below the horizon; a few moments ago it was still light enough to read but now it is no more, the printed characters swarm over the page to create an impressionistic blur. Soon the page itself will be invisible. Yet one has no urge to get up and put on a light; it is enough to be sitting here, grateful for the reminder that yet another day has come and gone, and you have done nothing about it. What about the morning resolutions to convert all the confused details in the air about you into a column of intelligible figures? To draw up a balance sheet? This naturally went undone, and you are perhaps grateful also for your laziness, glad that it has brought you to this pass where you must now face up to the day's inexorable end as indeed we must all face up to death some day, and put our faith in some superior power which will carry us beyond into a region of light and timelessness. Even if we had done the things we ought to have done it probably wouldn't have mattered anyway as everyone always leaves something undone and this can be just as ruinous as a whole life of crime or dissipation. Yes, in the long run there is something to be said for these shiftless days, each distilling its drop of poison until the cup is full; there is something to be said for them because there is no escaping them.

On the streets, in private places, they have no idea of the importance of these things. This exists only in our own minds, that is not in any place, nowhere. Possibly then it does not exist. Even its details are hazardous to consider. Most people would not consider it in its details, because (a) they would argue that details, no matter how complete, can give no adequate idea of the whole, and (b), because the details can too easily become fetishes, i.e., become prized for themselves, with no notion of the whole of which they were a part, with only an idolatrous understanding of the qualities of the particular detail. Certainly even this limited understanding can lead to a conception of beauty, insofar as any detail is a microcosm of the whole, as is so often the case. Thus you find people whose perfect understanding of love is deduced from lust, as the description of a flower can generate an idea of what it looks like. It is even possible that this irregular but satisfying understanding is the only one really allotted to us; that knowledge of the whole is impossible or at least so impractical as to be rarely or never feasible; that as we are born among imperfections we are indeed obligated to use them toward an assimilation of the imperfections that we are and the greater ones that we are to become; that not to do so would be to sin against nature, that is to end up with nothing, not even the reassuring knowledge that we have sinned to some purpose, but are instead empty and blameless as an inanimate object. Yet we know not what we are to become, therefore we can never completely rule out the possibility of intellectual understanding, even though it seems nothing but a snare and a delusion; we might miss out on everything by ignoring its call to order, which is in fact audible to each of us; therefore how can we decide? It is no solution either to combine the two approaches, to borrow from right reason or sensory data as the case seems to warrant, for an amalgam is not completeness either, and indeed is far less likely to be so through an error in dosage. So of the three methods: reason, sense, or a knowing combination of both, the last seems the least like a winner, the second problematic; only the first has some slim chance of succeeding through sheer perversity, which is possibly the only way to succeed at all. Thus we may be spared at least the agonizing wading through a slew of details of theories of action at the risk of getting hopelessly bogged down in them: better the erratic approach, which wins all or at least loses nothing, than the cautious semi-failure; better Don Quixote and his windmills than all the Sancho Panzas in the world; and may it not eventually turn out that to risk all is to win all, even at the expense of intimate, visceral knowledge of the truth, of its graininess and contours, even though this approach leads despite its physicality to no practical understanding of the truth, no grasp of how to use it toward ends it never dreams of? This, then, is surely the way; but discovery of where it begins is another matter.

The great careers are like that: a slow burst that narrows to a final release, pointed but not acute, a life of suffering redeemed and annihilated at the end, and for what? For a casual moment of knowing that is here one minute and gone the next, almost before you were aware of it? Whole tribes of seekers of phenomena who mattered very much to themselves have gone up in smoke in the space of a few seconds, with less fuss than a shooting star. Is it then that our bodies combined in such a way as to show others that we really mean it to each other—is this really all we ever intended to do? Having been born with knowledge or at least with the capacity to judge, to spend all our time working toward a way to show off that knowledge, so as to be able to return to it at the end for what it is? Besides the obvious question of who knows whether it will still be there, there is the even more urgent one of whose life are we taking into our hands? Is there no way in which these things may be done for themselves, so that others may enjoy them? Already we have wandered far from the track and, as always happens in such cases, darkness has fallen and it would be impossible to find one's way back without getting lost. Is this a reason to stay where we are, on the false assumption that we are less lost right here, and thus to complete the cycle of inertia that we began wrongly supposing that it would lead to knowledge? No, it is far better to continue on our way, even at the risk of getting more lost (an impossibility, of course). We might at least wind up with a knowledge of who *they* are, with whom we began, and at the very least with a new respect toward the others, reached through a more perfect understanding of ourselves and the true way. But still the "career" notion intervenes. It is impossible for us at the present time not to think of these people as separate entities, each with his development and aim to be achieved, careers which will "peak" after a while and then go back to being ordinary lives that fade quite naturally into air as they are used up, and are as though they never were, except for the "lesson" which has added an iota to the sum of all human understanding. And this way of speaking has trapped each one of us.

An alternative way would be the "life-as-ritual" concept. According to this theory no looking back is possible, in itself a considerable advantage, and the stages of the ritual are each considered in themselves, for themselves, but here no danger of fetichism is possible because all contact with the past has been severed. Fetichism comes into being only when there is a past that may seem more or less attractive when compared with the present; the resulting inequality causes a rush toward the immediate object of contemplation, hardens it into a husk around its own being, which promptly ceases. But the ritual approach provides some bad moments too. All its links severed with the worldly matrix from which it sprang, the soul feels that it is propelling itself forward at an ever-increasing speed. This very speed becomes a source of intoxication and of more gradually accruing speed; in the end the soul cannot recognize itself and is as one lost, though it imagines it has found eternal rest. But the true harmony which would render this peace interesting is lacking. There is only a cold knowledge of goodness and nakedness radiating out in every direction like the spines of the horse chestnut; mere knowledge and experience without the visual irregularities, those celestial motes in the eye that alone can transform ecstasy into a particular state beyond the dearly won generality. Here again, if backward looks were possible, not nostalgia but a series of carefully selected views, hieratic as icons, the difficulty would be eased and self could merge with selflessness, in a true appreciation of the tremendous volumes of eternity. But this is impossible because the ritual is by definition something impersonal, and can only move further in that direction. It was born without a knowledge of the past. And any attempt to hybridize it can only result in destruction and even death.

In addition to these twin notions of growth, two kinds of happiness are possible: the frontal and the latent. The first occurs naturally throughout life; it is experienced as a kind of sense of immediacy, even urgency; often we first become aware of it at a moment when we feel we need outside help. Its sudden balm suffuses the soul without warning, as a kind of bloom or grace. We suppose that souls "in glory" feel this way permanently, as a day-to-day condition of being: yes, as a condition, for it is both more and less than a state; it exacts certain prerequisites and then it builds on these, but the foundation is never forgotten; it is the foundation that is happiness. And as it exacts, so it bestows. There is not the mindlessness, no idea of eternal lassitude permeated with the light of the firmament or whatever; there are only the value judgments of truth, exposed one after another like colored slides on the white wall that is the naked soul, or a kind of hard glaze that definitively transforms the ordinary clay of the soul into an object of beauty by obliterating the knowledge of what lies underneath. This is what we are all hoping for, yet we know that very few among us will ever achieve it; those who do will succeed less through their own efforts than through the obscure workings of grace as chance, so that although we would be very glad to have the experience of this sudden opening up, this inundation which shall last an eternity, we do not bother our heads too much about it, so distant and far away it seems, like those beautiful mosaic ceilings representing heaven which we crane up at from below, knowing that we cannot get near enough for it to be legible but liking all the same the vastness and aura of the conception, glad to have seen it and to know it's there but nevertheless firmly passing outward into the sunlight after two or three turns around the majestic dim interior. This kind of beauty is almost too abstract to be experienced as beauty, and yet we must realize that it is not an abstract notion, that it really can happen at times and that life at these times seems marvelous. Indeed this is truly what we were brought into creation for, if not to experience it, at least to have the knowledge of it as an ideal toward which the whole universe tends and which therefore confers a shape on the random movements outside us— these are all straining in the same direction, toward the same goal, though it is certain that few if any of those we see now will attain it.

The second kind, the latent or dormant kind, is harder to understand. We all know those periods of balmy weather in early spring, sometimes even before spring has officially begun: days or even a few hours when the air seems suffused with an unearthly tenderness, as though love were about to start, now, at this moment, on an endless journey put off since the beginning of time. Just to walk a few steps in this romantic atmosphere is to experience a magical but quiescent bliss, as though the torch of life were about to be placed in one's hands: after having anticipated it for so long, what is one now to do? And so the happiness withholds itself, perhaps even indefinitely; it realizes that the vessel has not yet been fully prepared to receive it; it is afraid it will destroy the order of things by precipitating itself too soon. But this in turn quickens the dismay of the vessel or recipient; it, or we, have been waiting all our lives for this sign of fulfillment, now to be abruptly snatched away so soon as barely perceived. And a kind of panic develops, which for many becomes a permanent state of being, with all the appearances of a calm, purposeful, reflective life. These people are awaiting the sign of their felicity without hope; its *nearness* is there, tingeing the air around them, in suspension, in escrow as it were, but they cannot get at it. Yet so great is their eagerness that they believe that they have already absorbed it, that they have attained that plane of final realization which we are all striving for, that they have achieved a state of permanent grace. Hence the air of joyful resignation, the beatific upturned eyelids, the paralyzed stance of these castaways of the eternal voyage, who imagine they have reached the promised land when in reality the ship is sinking under them. The great fright has turned their gaze upward, to the stars, to the heavens; they see nothing of the disarray around them, their ears are closed to the cries of their fellow passengers; they can think only of themselves when all the time they believe that they are thinking of nothing but God. Yet in their innermost minds they know too that all is not well; that if it were there would not be this rigidity, with the eye and the mind focused on a nonexistent center, a fixed point, when the common sense of even an idiot would be enough to make him realize that nothing has stopped, that we and everything around us are moving forward continually, and that we are being modified constantly by the speed at which we travel and the regions through which we pass, so that merely to think of ourselves as having arrived at some final resting place is a contradiction of fundamental logic, since even the dullest of us knows enough to realize that he is ignorant of everything, including the basic issue of whether we are really moving at all or whether the concept of motion is something that can even be spoken of in connection with such ignorant beings as we, for whom the term ignorant is indeed perhaps an overstatement, implying as it does that something is known somewhere, whereas in reality we are not even sure of this: we in fact cannot aver with any degree of certainty that we *are* ignorant. Yet this is not so bad; we have at any rate kept our open-mindedness—*that*, at least, we may be sure that we have—and are not in any danger, or so it seems, of freezing into the pious attitudes of those true spiritual bigots whose faces are turned toward eternity and who therefore can see nothing. We know that we are en route in a certain sense, and also that there has been a hitch somewhere: we have as it were boarded the train but for some unexplained reason it has not yet started. But there is in this as yet only slight delay matter for concern even for the likes of us, intelligent and only modestly expectant as we are, patient, meek without any overtones of ironic resignation before a situation we are powerless to change and secretly believe is likely to go from bad to worse. There is nothing of that in us, we are not bigots and we have kept an open mind, we have all our mobility in a word, yet we too sense a danger and we do not quite know how we are going to react. Those first few steps, in the prematurely mild air that a blizzard is surely destined to dash from living memory before tomorrow comes—aren't we in danger of accepting these only for what they are, of being thankful for them and letting our gratitude take the place of further inquiry into what they were like, of letting it stand both for our attitude as eternity will view it and also for the fulfillment of which this was just the promise? That surely is the danger we run in our state of sophisticated but innocent enlightenment: that of not *demanding* and getting a hearing, of not finding out where these steps were leading even in the teeth of an almost dead certainty that it was nowhere, even of doubting that they ever took place, that any kind of structure or fabric in which they would assume being could ever have existed. So that in our way we are

worse off or at least in worse danger than those others who imagine them-
selves already delivered from the chain of rebirth. *They* have their illusions
to sustain them, even though these are full of holes and sometimes don't
prevent their possessors from feeling the chilly drafts of doubt, while we
can be brought to doubt that any of this, which we know in our heart of
hearts to be a real thing, an event of the highest spiritual magnitude, ever
happened. Here it is that our sensuality can save us *in extremis:* the atmo-
sphere of the day that event took place, the way the trees and buildings
looked, what we said to the person who was both the bearer and fellow
recipient of that message and what that person replied, words that were not
words but sounds out of time, taken out of any eternal context in which
their content would be recognizable—these facts have entered our con-
sciousness once and for all, have spread through us even into our pores like
a marvelous antidote to the cup that the next moment had already prepared
and which, whether hemlock or nectar, could only have proved fatal be-
cause it *was* the next, bringing with it the unspoken message that motion
could be accomplished only in time, that is in a preordained succession of
moments which must carry us far from here, far from this impassive but
real moment of understanding which may be the only one we shall ever
know, even if it is merely the first of an implied infinite series. But what if
this were all? What if it were true that "once is enough"? That all conse-
quences, all resonances of this singular event were to be cut off by virtue of
its very singularity; nay, that even for memory, insofar as it can profit
anyone, this instant were to be as though it had never existed, expunged
from the chronicles of recorded time, fallen lower than the last circle of hell
into a pit of total negation, and all this in our own best interests, so that we
might not be led astray into imagining its goodness infinitely extendible, a
thing that could never happen given the absolute and all-pervading nature
of that goodness, destined to occur only once in the not-to-be-repeated
cycle of eternity? Yet this seems not quite right, a little too pat perhaps,
and here again it is our senses that are of some use to us in distinguishing
verity from falsehood. For they never would have been able to capture the
emanations from that special point of life if they were not meant to do
something with them, weave them into the pattern of the days that come

after, sunlit or plunged in shadow as they may be, but each with the identifying scarlet thread that runs through the whole warp and woof of the design, sometimes almost disappearing in its dark accretions, but at others emerging as the full inspiration of the plan of the whole, grandly organizing its repeated vibrations and imposing its stamp on these until the meaning of it all suddenly flashes out of the shimmering pools of scarlet like a vast and diaphanous though indestructible framework, not to be lost sight of again? And here we may say that even if the uniqueness were meant to last only the duration of its unique instant, which I don't for a moment believe, but let us assume so for the sake of argument—even if this were the case, its aura would still be meant to linger on in our days, informing us of and gently prodding us toward the right path, even though we might correctly consider ourselves shut off from the main source, never to be in a position to contemplate its rightness again, yet despite this able to consider its traces in the memory as a supreme good, as a god come down to earth to instruct us in the ways of the other kingdom, for he sees that we have not progressed very far on our own—no farther than those first few steps in the suddenly mild open air. And we are lucky that he chooses so to deal with us, for as of this moment our worries are over, we have only to step forward to be in the right path, we are all walking in it and we always have been, only we never knew it. The end is still shrouded in mystery, but the mystery diminishes without exactly becoming clearer the more we advance, like a city whose plan begins to take shape on the horizon as we approach it, yet that is not precisely the case here because we certainly perceive no more of the divine enigma as we progress, it is just that its mystery lessens and comes to seem, whenever we stop to think of it which is not very often, the least important feature of the whole. What does matter is our growing sense of certainty, whether deduced by the intellect or the sensual intelligence (this is immaterial): it is there, and this is all we need bother about, just as there is no need to examine a man's ancestry or antecedents in evaluating his personal qualities. But, after the question of how did it get there, which we now perceive to be futile, another question remains: how are we to use it? Not only by what means, which is an important enough consideration, but toward what end? Toward our own betterment and by extension that of the world around us or conversely toward the improvement of the world, which we might believe would incidentally render us as its citizens better people, even though this were just a side effect? The answer is in our morning waking. For just as we begin our lives as mere babes with the imprint of nothing in our heads, except lingering traces of a previous existence which grow fainter and fainter as we progress until we have forgotten them entirely, only by this time other notions have imposed themselves so that our infant minds are never a complete *tabula rasa*, but there is always something fading out or just coming into focus, and this whatever-it-is is always projecting itself on us, escalating its troops, prying open the shut gates of our sensibility and pouring in to augment its forces that have begun to take over our naked consciousness and driving away those shreds of another consciousness (although not, perhaps, forever—nothing is permanent—but perhaps until our last days when their forces shall again mass on the borders of our field of perception to remind us of that other old existence which we are now called to rejoin) so that for a moment, between the fleeing and the pursuing armies there is almost a moment of peace, of purity in which what we are meant to perceive could almost take shape in the empty air, if only there were time enough, and yet in the time it takes to perceive the dimness of its outline we can if we are quick enough seize the meaning of that assurance, before returning to the business at hand—just, I say, as we begin each day in this state of threatened blankness which is wiped away so soon, but which leaves certain illegible traces, like chalk dust on a blackboard after it has been erased, so we must learn to recognize it as the form—the only one—in which such fragments of the true learning as we are destined to receive will be vouchsafed to us, if at all. The unsatisfactoriness, the frowns and squinting, the itching and scratching as you listen without taking in what is being said to you, or only in part, so that you cannot piece the argument together, should not be dismissed as signs of our chronic all-too-human weakness but welcomed and examined as signs of life in which part of the whole truth lies buried. And as the discourse continues and you think you are not getting anything out of it, as you yawn and rub your eyes and pick your nose or scratch your head, or nudge your neighbor on the hard wooden bench, this knowledge is getting through to you, and taking just the forms it needs to impress itself upon you, the forms of your inattention and incapacity or unwillingness to understand. For it is certain that you will rise from the bench a new person, and even before you have emerged into the full daylight of the street you will feel that a change has begun to operate in you, within your very fibers and sinews, and when the light of the street floods over you it will have become real at last, all traces of doubt will have been pulverized by the influx of light slowly mounting to bury those crass seamarks of egocentricity and warped self-esteem you were able to navigate by but which you no longer need now that the rudder has been swept out of your hands, and this whole surface of daylight has become one with that other remembered picture of light, when you were setting out, and which you feared would disappear because of its uniqueness, only now realizing that this singleness was the other side of the coin of its many-faceted diversity and interest, and that it may be simultaneously cherished for the former and lived in thanks to the versatility of the latter. It may be eaten, and breathed, and it would indeed have no reason to exist if this were not the case. So I think that the question of how we are going to use the reality of our revelation, as well as to what end, has now been resolved. First of all we see that these two aspects of our question are actually one and the same, that there is only one aspect as well as only one question, that to wonder how is the same as beginning to know why. For no choice is possible. In the early moments of wondering after the revelation had been received it could have been that this way of doing seemed to promise more, that that one had already realized its potential, that therefore there was matter for hesitation and the possibility of loss between a way that had already proved itself and another, less sure one that could lead to greener pastures, to cloud-cuckoo land and even farther, just because the implied risk seemed to posit a greater virtue in the acceptance. But it is certain now that these two ways are the same, that we *have* them both, the risk and the security, merely through being human creatures subject to the vicissitudes of time, our earthly lot. So that this second kind of happiness is merely a fleshed-out, realized version of that ideal first kind, and more to be prized because its now ripe contours enfold both the promise and the shame of our human state, which they therefore proceed to transmute into something that is an amalgam of both, the faithful reflection of the idealistic concept that got us started along this path, but a reflection which is truer than the original because more suited to us, and whose shining perspectives we can feel and hold, clenching the journey to us like the bread and meat left by the wayside for the fatigued traveler by an anonymous Good Samaritan—ourselves, perhaps, just as Hop-o'-My-Thumb distributed crumbs along the way to guide him back in the dark, only these the birds have miraculously spared: they are ours. To know this is to be able to relax without any danger of becoming stagnant. Thus the difficulty of living with the unfolding of the year is erased, the preparing for spring and then for the elusive peace of summer, followed by the invigorating readjustments of autumn and the difficult and never very successful business of adapting to winter and the approach of another year. This way we are automatically attuned to these progressions and can forget about them; what matters is us and not what time makes of us, or rather it is what we make of ourselves that matters. What is this? Just the absorption of ourselves seen from the outside, when it is really what is going on inside us—all this overheard chatter and speculation and the noises of the day as it wears on into the calm of night, joyful or abysmal as it may be: this doesn't matter once we have accepted it and taken it inside us to be the interior walls of our chamber, the place where we live. And so all these conflicting meaningless details are transformed into something peaceful that surrounds, like wallpaper that could be decorated with scenes of shipwrecks or military attributes or yawning crevasses in the earth and which doesn't matter, which indeed can paradoxically heighten the feeling of a peaceful domestic interior. Yet this space wasn't made just for the uses of peace, but also for action, for planned assaults on the iniquity and terror outside, though this doesn't mean either that we shall have at some point to go outside or on the contrary that our plans will remain at the stage of dreams or armies in the fire: we carry both inside and outside around with us as we move purposefully toward an operation that is going to change us on every level, and is also going to alter the balance of power of happiness in the world in our favor and that of all the human beings in the world. And how is this to become possible? Let us assume for the sake of argument that the blizzard I spoke of earlier has occurred, shattering the frail décor of your happiness like a straw house, replunging you and your world into the gray oblivion you had been floundering in all your life until the day your happiness was given to you as a gift, a reward or so it seemed for the stale unprofitable journey you called your life, only now it seemed that it was just beginning, and at the same moment you had an impression of stopping or ending. Apparently then happiness was to be a fixed state, but then you perceived that it was both fixed and mobile at the same time, like a fixed source of light with rays running out from and connecting back to it. This suited you very well, because it replied to your twin urges to act and to remain at peace with yourself and with the warring elements outside. And now these have again taken over and crushed your fragile dream of happiness, so that it all seems meaningless. Gazing out at the distraught but inanimate world you feel that you have lapsed back into the normal way things are, that what you were feeling just now was a novelty and hence destined to disappear quickly, its sole purpose if any being to light up the gloom around you sufficiently for you to become aware of its awesome extent, more than the eye and the mind can take in. The temptation here is to resume the stoic pose, tinged with irony and self-mockery, of times before. There was no point in arriving at this place, but neither, you suppose, would there have been any in avoiding it. It is all the same to you. And you turn away from the window almost with a sense of relief, to bury yourself again in the task of sorting out the jumbled scrap basket of your recent days, without any hope of completing it or even caring whether it gets done or not. But you find that you are unable to pick up the threads where you left off; the details of things shift and their edges swim before your tired eyes; it is impossible to make even the rudimentary sense of them that you once could. You see that you cannot do without it, that singular isolated moment that has now already slipped so far into the past that it seems a mere spark. You cannot do without it and you cannot have it. At this point a drowsiness overtakes you as of total fatigue and indifference; in this unnatural, dreamy state the objects you have been contemplating take on a life of their own, in and for themselves. It seems to you that you are eavesdropping and can understand their private language. They are not talking about you at all, but are telling each other curious private stories about things you can only half comprehend, and other things that have a meaning only for themselves and are beyond any kind of understanding. And these in turn would know other sets of objects, limited to their own perceptions and at the limit of the scope of visibility of those that discuss them and dream about them. It could be that time and space are filled up with these to infinity and beyond; that there is no such thing as a void, only endless lists of things that may or may not be aware of one another, the "sad variety of woe." And this pointless diversity plunges you into a numbing despair and blankness. The whole world seems dyed the same melancholy hue. Nothing in it can arouse your feelings. Even the sun seems dead. And all because you succumbed to what seemed an innocent and perfectly natural craving, to have your cake and eat it too, forgetting that, widespread as it is, it cannot be excused on any human grounds because it cannot be realized. Therefore even to contemplate it is a sin. But, you say, in those first moments . . . Never mind that now. You must forget them. The dream that was fleetingly revealed to you was a paradox, and for this reason must be forgotten as quickly as possible. But, you continue to argue, it mattered precisely because it was a paradox and about to be realized here on earth, in human terms; otherwise one would have forgotten it as quickly as any morning dream that clings to you in the first few waking moments, until its incongruities become blatant in the reasonable daylight that seeps back into your consciousness. It was not a case of a spoiled child asking its mother for something for the nth time or of wishing on a star; it was a *new arrangement* that existed and was on the point of working. And now it is all the same; any miracles, if there ever are any again, will be partial ones, mere virtuosic exhibitions beside the incontrovertible reality of that other, as amazingly real as a new element or a new dimension. And so it goes. But if it was indeed as real as all that, then it *was* real, and therefore it *is* real. Just as matter cannot be added to or subtracted from the universe, or energy destroyed, so with something real, that is, real in the sense you understood it and understand it. When will you realize that your dreams have eternal life? I of course don't mean that you are a moonstruck dreamer, but that they do exist, outside of you, without your having to do anything about it. Even if you do something it won't matter. And it is possible that you will always remain unaware of their existence; this won't matter either, to them, that is. But you must try to seize the truth of this: whatever was, is, and must be. The darkness that surrounds you now does not exist, because it never had any independent existence: you created it out of the spleen and torment you felt. It looks real enough to hide you from the light of the sun, but its reality is as specious as that of a mirage. The clouds are dispersing. And nothing comes to take their place, to interpose itself between you and the reality which you dreamed and which is therefore real. This new arrangement is already guiding your steps and indicating the direction you should take without your realizing it, for it is invisible now; it still seems that it is lost for there is of course no tangible evidence of it: *that* happens only once, it is true. But now to have absorbed the lesson, to have recovered from the shock of not being able to remember it, to again be setting out from the beginning— is this not something good to you? You no longer have to remember the principles, they seem to come to you like fragments of a buried language you once knew. You are like the prince in the fairy tale before whom the impenetrable forest opened and then the gates of the castle, without his knowing why. The one thing you want is to pause so as to puzzle all this out, but that is impossible; you are moving much too quickly for your momentum to be halted. How will it all turn out? What will the end be? But these are questions of the ignorant novice which you have forgotten about already. You think now only in terms of the speed with which you advance, and which you drink in like oxygen; it has become the element in which you live and which is you. Nothing else matters.

And so, not bothering about anything, you again took things into your own hands. You were a little incredulous as to the outcome, but you decided to try it anyway. Who could tell what would happen? It didn't do to dwell too much on those ideal forms of happiness that had haunted you ever since the cradle and had now defined themselves almost in a paroxysm; they could be assigned to the corners and cubbyholes of your mind since it didn't matter whether they were in evidence as long as you never actually lost sight of them. What did matter now was getting down to business, or back to the business of day-to-day living with all the tiresome mechanical problems that this implies. And it was just here that philosophy broke down completely and was of no use. How to deal with the new situations that arise each day in bunches or clusters, and which resist categorization to the point where any rational attempt to deal with them is doomed from the start? And in particular how to deal with this one that faces you now, which has probably been with you always; now it has a different name and a different curriculum vitae; its qualities are combined in such a way as to seem different from all that has gone before, but actually it is the same old surprise that you have always lived with. Forget about the details of name and place, forget also the concepts and archetypes that haunt you and which are as much a part of the typical earthbound situation you find yourself in as those others: neither the concept nor the state of affairs logically deduced from it is going to be of much help to you now. What is required is the ability to enter into the complexities of the situation as though it really weren't new at all, which it isn't, as one takes the first few steps into a labyrinth. Here one abruptly finds one's intuition tailored to the needs of the new demanding syndrome; each test is passed flawlessly, as though in a dream, and the complex climate that is formed by the vacillating wills and energies of the many who surround you becomes as easy as pie for you. You take on all comers but you do not advertise your presence. Right now it is important to slip as quickly as possible into the Gordian contours of the dank, barren morass (or so it seems at present) without uttering so much as a syllable; to live in that labyrinth that seems to be directing your steps but in reality it is you who are creating its pattern, embarked on a new, fantastically difficult tactic whose success is nevertheless guaranteed. You know this. But it will be a long time before the ordinary assurances will be able to make themselves felt in the strange, closed-off state you are in now. You may as well forget them and abandon yourself to the secret growing that has taken over. Nothing can stop it, so there is no point in worrying about it or even thinking about it.

How we move around in our little ventilated situation, how roomy it seems! There is so much to do after all, so many people to be with, and we like them all. But meanwhile it seems as if our little space were moving counter to us, dragging us backward. We have reached this far point of where we are by following someone's advice, and at times it seems as though it might have been the wrong advice. If this were the case, to become aware of it would be no help because we have refined the baser elements out of our present situation and are technically on the same footing with others of different origins who meet and socialize with us. One sign of this is that no one remarks on the lateness of the hour, for we all believe we have reached a point where such details no longer count; we believe that we are immune to time because we are "out of" it. Yet we know dimly that the stillness we have attained is racing forward faster than ever toward its rendezvous with the encroaching past; we know this and we turn from it, to take refuge in dreams where all is not exactly well either, in which we reach the summit of our aspirations to find the mass below riddled and honeycombed with vacancy, yet there is room on the crest to move around in; it might almost qualify as an oasis. But as we all know, the thing about an oasis is that the whole desert has to become one before its exotic theories can benefit us, and even that would not be enough because then there would be too much of a contrast with the ordinary temperate climate leading up to it. Yet one can very well live and enjoy the fruits of one's considerable labors in arriving at this place which could be the end of the world in no unfavorable sense; there are the same things to look at and be surrounded by although in lesser numbers; what it is is quality as opposed to quantity. But can the one exist without the other? These thoughts oppress one in the social world one has built around oneself, especially the thought of those other infinite worlds upon worlds; and when one really examines one's own world in the harsher light of its happiness-potential one sees that it is a shambles indeed. Yet there is air to breathe. One may at least stay here a while hoping for more and better things to come.

That's the way it goes. For many weeks you have been exploring what seemed to be a profitable way of doing. You discovered that there was a fork in the road, so first you followed what seemed to be the less promising, or at any rate the more obvious, of the two branches until you felt you had a good idea of where it led. Then you returned to investigate the more tangled way, and for a time its intricacies seemed to promise a more complex and therefore a more practical goal for you, one that could be picked up in any number of ways so that all its faces or applications could be thoroughly scrutinized. And in so doing you began to realize that the two branches were joined together again, farther ahead; that this place of joining was indeed the end, and that it was the very place you set out from, whose intolerable mixture of reality and fantasy had started you on the road which has now come full circle. It has been an absorbing puzzle, but in the end all the pieces fit together like a ghost story that turns out to have a perfectly rational explanation. Nothing remains but to begin living with this discovery, that is, without the hope mentioned above. Even this is not so easy, for the reduced mode or scope must itself be nourished by a form of hope, or hope that doesn't take itself seriously. One must move very fast in order to stay in the same place, as the Red Queen said, the reason being that once you have decided there is no alternative to remaining motionless you must still learn to cope with the onrushing tide of time and all the confusing phenomena it bears in its wake, some of which perfectly resemble the unfinished but seemingly salvageable states of reality at cross-purposes with itself that first caused you to grow restless, to begin fidgeting with various impractical schemes that were in the end, we have seen, finally reduced to zero. Yet they cannot be banished from the system any more than physical matter can, and their nature, which is part and parcel of their existence, is to remain incomplete, clamoring for wholeness. So that now two quite other and grimmer alternatives present themselves: that of staying where you are and risking eventual destruction at the hands of those dishonest counselors of many aspects, or of being swept back by them into a past drenched in nostalgia whose sweetness burns like gall. And it is a choice that we have to make.

As a lost dog on the edge of a sidewalk timidly approaches first one passerby and then another, uncertain of what to ask for, taking a few embarrassed steps in one direction and then suddenly veering to another before being able to ascertain what reception his mute entreaty might have met with, lost, puzzled, ashamed, ready to slink back into his inner confusion at the first brush with the outside world, so your aspirations, my soul, on this busy thoroughfare that is the great highway of life. What do you think to gain from merely standing there looking worried, while the tide of humanity sweeps ever onward, toward some goal it gives every sign of being as intimately acquainted with as you are with the sharp-edged problems that beset you from every angle? Do you really think that if you succeed in looking pathetic enough some kindly stranger will stop to ask your name and address and then steer you safely to your very door? No, I do not think you are afflicted with that kind of presumption, and yet your pitiable waif's stance, that inquiring look that darts uneasily from side to side as though to ward off a blow—these do not argue in your favor, even though we both know you to be a strong upright character, far above such cheap attempts to play on the emotions of others. And there is no use trying to tell them that the touching melancholy of your stare is the product not of self-pity but of a lucid attempt to find out just where you stand in the fast-moving stream of traffic that flows endlessly from horizon to horizon like a dark river. We know that the pose you happen to be striking for the world to see matters nothing to you, it could just as easily be some other one, joyous-looking or haughty and overbearing, or whatever. It is only that you happened to be wearing this look as you arrived at the end of your perusal of the way left open to you, and it "froze" on you, just as your mother warned you it would when you were little. And now it is the face you show to the world, the face of expectancy, strange as it seems. Perhaps Childe Roland wore such a look as he drew nearer to the Dark Tower, every energy concentrated toward the encounter with the King of Elfland, reasonably certain of the victorious outcome, yet not so much as to erase the premature lines of care from his pale and tear-stained face. Maybe it is just that you don't want to outrage anyone, especially now that the moment of your own encounter seems to be getting closer. You can

feel it in every pore, in the sudden hush that falls over the din of the busy
street and the unusual darkness in the sky even though no clouds are
apparent. Your miserable premature spring has finally turned into the real
thing, confirmed by the calendar, but what a sad look it wears, especially
after its promising beginnings that now seem so far back in the past. The
air is moist and almost black, and sharp with the chill; the magnolia petals
flatten and fall off one after the other onto the half-frozen mud of the
ground where only a few spears of sickly green grass have managed to lift
their heads. All this comes as no surprise, it is even somewhat of a relief,
and better than the dire sequel that those precocious moments seemed to
promise, cataclysms instead of the ominous hush that now lies over every-
thing. And who is to say whether or not this silence isn't the very one you
requested so as to be able to speak? Perhaps it seems ominous only because
it is concentrating so intensely on you and what you have to say.

"Whatever was, is, and must be"—these words occur again to you now,
though in a different register, transposed from a major into a minor key. Yet
they are the same words as before. Their meaning is the same, only you
have changed: you are viewing it all from a different angle, perhaps not
more nor less accurate than the previous one, but in any case a necessary
one no doubt for the in-the-round effect to be achieved. We see it all now.
The thing that our actions have accomplished, and its results for us. And it
is no longer a nameless thing, but something colorful and full of interest, a
chronicle play of our lives, with the last act still in the dim future, so that
we can't tell yet whether it is a comedy or a tragedy, all we know is that it
is crammed with action and the substance of life. Surely all this living that
has gone on that is ours is good in some way, though we cannot tell why:
we know only that our sympathy has deepened, quickened by the onrush-
ing spectacle, to the point where we are like spectators swarming up onto
the stage to be absorbed into the play, though always aware that this is an
impossibility, and that the actors continue to recite their lines as if we
weren't there. Yet in the end, we think, this may become possible; that is
the time when audience and actor and writer and director all mingle joy-

ously together as one, as the curtain descends a last time to separate them from the half-empty theater. When this happens—yet there is no point in looking to that either. The apotheosis never attracted you, only those few moments in the next-to-last act where everything suddenly becomes momentarily clear, to sink again into semi-obscurity before the final blaze which merely confirms the truth of what had been succinctly stated long before. But there does not seem to be any indication that this moment is approaching.

Except that the silence continues to focus on you. Who am I after all, you say despairingly once again, to have merited so much attention on the part of the universe; what does it think to get from me that it doesn't have already? I know too that my solipsistic approach is totally wrongheaded and foolish, that the universe isn't listening to me any more than the sea can be heard inside conch shells. But I'm just a mute observer—it isn't my fault that I can really notice how everything around me is waiting just for me to get up and say the word, whatever that is. And surely even the eyes of the beloved are fixed on you as though wondering, "What is he going to do *this* time?" And those eyes as well as the trees and skies that surround you are full of apprehension, waiting for this word that must come from you and that you have not in you. "What am I going to say?" But as you continue gazing embarrassedly into the eyes of the beloved, talking about extraneous matters, you become aware of an invisible web that connects those eyes to you, and both of you to the atmosphere of this room which is leading up to you after the vagaries of the space outside. Suddenly you realize that you have been talking for a long time without listening to yourself; you must have said *it* a long way back without knowing it, for everything in the room has fallen back into its familiar place, only this time organized according to the invisible guidelines that radiate out from both of you like the laws that govern a kingdom. Now there is so much to talk about that it seems neither of you will ever get done talking. And the word that everything hinged on is buried back there; by mutual consent neither of you examined it when it was pronounced and rushed to its final resting place. It is doing the organizing, the guidelines radiate from its control; therefore it is good not to know what it is since its results can be known so intimately, appreciated for what they are; it is best then that the buried word remain buried for we were intended to appreciate only its fruits and not the secret principle activating them—to know this would be to know too much. Meanwhile it is possible to know just enough, and this is all we were supposed to know, toward which we have been straining all our lives. We are to read this in outward things: the spoons and greasy tables in this room, the wooden shelves, the flyspecked ceiling merging into gloom— good and happy things, nevertheless, that tell us little of themselves and more about ourselves than we had ever imagined it was possible to know. They have become the fabric of life.

Until, accustomed to disappointments, you can let yourself rule and be ruled by these strings or emanations that connect everything together, you haven't fully exorcised the demon of doubt that sets you in motion like a rocking horse that cannot stop rocking. You may have scored a few points there where you first took those few steps (no more than three, in all likelihood) when you first realized the enormity of the choice between two kinds of mutually exclusive universal happiness. And you also realized the error of forever ruminating on and repeating those fatal steps, like a broken movie projector that keeps showing the same strip of film—you realized this when you were already far from that experience which had indeed begun to take on the unearthly weirdness of an old photograph. You cried out in the desert and you collapsed into yourself, indifferent to the progress of the seasons and the planets in their orbits, and you died for the first time. And now that you have been raised from the tomb like Lazarus by obscure miraculous forces you are surprised that the earth isn't better than the one you left behind, that all things haven't yet perfected themselves as you believe you have done by dying and being resuscitated to the uncertain glory of this day in early spring. You can't get over the fact that conversations still sound the same, that clouds of unhappiness still persist in the unseen mesh that draws around everything, uniting it in a firm purpose as

153

it causes each individual thing to bulge more brightly and more darkly at the same time, drawing out the nature of its real being. But that is the wonder of it: that you have returned not to the supernatural glow of heaven but to the ordinary daylight you knew so well before it passed from your view, and which continues to enrich you as it steeps you and your ageless chattels of mind, imagination, timid first love and quiet acceptance of experience in its revitalizing tide. And the miracle is not that you have returned—you always knew you would—but that things have remained the same. The day is not far advanced: it still half-seriously offers with one hand the promise that it pockets with the other, and it is still up to you to seize the occasion, jump into the fray, not be ruled by its cruel if only human whims. The person sitting opposite you who asked you a question is still waiting for the answer; he has not yet found your hesitation unusual, but it is up to you to grasp it with both hands, wrenching it from the web of connectives to rub off the grime that has obscured its brilliance so as to restore it to him, that pause which is the answer you have both been expecting. When it was new everybody could tell this, but years of inactivity and your own inattention have tarnished it beyond recognition. It needs a new voice to tell it, otherwise it will seem just another awkward pause in a conversation largely made up of similar ones, and will never be able to realize its potential as a catalyst, turning you both in on yourself and outward to that crystalline gaze that has been the backing of your days and nights for so long now. For the time being only you know it for what it is, but as you continue to hold on to it others will begin to realize its true nature, until finally it stands as the shortest distance between your aims and those of the beloved, the only human ground that can nurture your hopes and fears into the tree of life that is as big as the universe and entirely fills it up with its positive idea of growth and gaining control. So it is permissible to rest here awhile in this pause you alone discovered: a little repose can do no harm at this stage; meanwhile do not fear that when you next speak the whole scene will come to life again, as though triggered by invisible machines. There is not much for you to do except wait in the anticipation of your inevitable reply.

Inevitable, but so often postponed. Whole eras of history have sprung up in the gaps left by these pauses, dynasties, barbarian invasions and so on until the grass and shards stage, and still the answer is temporarily delayed. During these periods one thought enclosed everything like the blue sky of history: that it really was this one and no other. As long as this is the case everything else can take its course, time can flow into eternity leaving a huge deltalike deposit whose fan broadens and broadens and is my life, the time I am taking; we get up in the morning and blow on some half-dead coals, maybe for the last time; my hair is white and straggly and I hardly recognize my face any more, yet none of this matters so long as your reply twists it all together, the transparent axle of this particular chapter in history. It seems that the blue of the sky is a little paler each morning, as happens toward the end of each epoch, yet one doesn't want to move hastily, but to continue at this half-savage, half-pastoral existence, until one day the unmistakable dry but deep accent is heard:

"You waited too long. And now you are going to be rewarded by my attention. Make no mistake: it will probably seem to you as though nothing has changed; nothing will show in the outward details of your life and each night you will creep tired and enraged into bed. Know however that I am listening. From now on the invisible bounty of my concern will be there to keep you company, and as you mature it will unlock more of the same space for you so that eventually all your territory will have become right- fully yours again."

I know now that I am no longer waiting, and that the previous part of my life in which I thought I was waiting and therefore only half-alive was not waiting, although it was tinged with expectancy, but living under and into this reply which has suddenly caused everything in my world to take on new meaning. It is as though I had picked up a thread which I had merely mislaid but which for a long time seemed lost. And all because I am certain now, albeit for no very good reason, that it was this one and no other. The sadness that infected us as children and stayed on through adulthood has healed, and there can be no other way except this way of health we are taking, silent as it is. But it lets us look back on those other, seemingly spoiled days and re-evaluate them: actually they were too well-rounded, each bore its share of happiness and grief and finished its tale just as twilight was descending; those days are now an inseparable part of our story despite their air of immaturity and tentativeness; they have the freshness of early works which may be wrongly discarded later. Nor is today really any different: we are as childish as ever, it turns out, only perhaps a little better at disguising it, but we still want what we want when we want it and no power on earth is strong enough to deny it to us. But at least we see now that this is how things are, and so we have the sense to stop insisting every so often under the guise of some apparently unrelated activity, because we think we shall be better satisfied this way; underneath the discreet behavior the desire is as imperious as ever, but after so many postponements we now realize that a little delay won't hurt and we can relax in the assurance of eventual satisfaction. This was the message of that day in the street, when you first perceived that conventional happiness would not do for you and decided to opt for the erratic kind despite the dangers that its need for continual growth and expansion exposed it to. This started you on your way, although it often seemed as though your feet had struck roots into the ground and you were doomed to grow and decay like a tree. Nevertheless you were aware of moving, whether it was you who were moving or the landscape moving forward toward you, and you could remain patient with the idea of growth as long as the concept of uniqueness—that one and no other—shone like a star in the sky above you.

Today your wanderings have come full circle. Having begun by rejecting the idea of oneness in favor of a plurality of experiences, earthly and spiritual, in fact a plurality of different lives that you lived out to your liking while time proceeded at another, imperturbable rate, you gradually became aware that the very diversity of these experiences was endangered by its own inner nature, for variety implies parallelism, and all these highly individualistic ways of thinking and doing were actually moving in the same direction and constantly threatening to merge with one another in a single one-way motion toward that invisible goal of concrete diversity. For just as all kinds of people spring up on earth and imagine themselves very different from each other though they are basically the same, so all these ideas had arisen in the same head and were merely aspects of a single organism: yourself, or perhaps your desire to be different. So that now in order to avoid extinction it again became necessary to invoke the idea of oneness, only this time if possible on a higher plane, in order for the similarities in your various lives to cancel each other out and the differences to remain, but under the aegis of singleness, separateness, so that each difference might be taken as the type of all the others and yet remain intrinsically itself, unlike anything in the world. Which brings us to you and the scene in the little restaurant. You are still there, far above me like the polestar and enclosing me like the dome of the heavens; your singularity has become oneness, that is your various traits and distinguishing marks have flattened out into a cloudlike protective covering whose irregularities are all functions of its uniformity, and which constitutes an arbitrary but definitive boundary line between the new informal, almost haphazard way of life that is to be mine permanently and the monolithic samenesses of the world that exists to be shut out. For it has been measured once and for all. It would be wrong to look back at it, and luckily we are so constructed that the urge to do so can never waken in us. We are both alive and free.

If you could see a movie of yourself you would realize that this is true. Movies show us ourselves as we had not yet learned to recognize us—something in the nature of daily being or happening that quickly gets folded over into ancient history like yesterday's newspaper, but in so doing a new face has been revealed, a surface on which a new phrase may be written before it rejoins history, or it may remain blank and do so anyway: it doesn't matter because each thing is coming up in its time and receding into the past, and this is what we all expect and want. What does matter is what becomes of it once it has entered the past's sacred precincts; when, bending under the weight of an all-powerful nostalgia, its every contour is at last revealed for what it was, but this can be known only in the past. It isn't wrong to look at things in this way—how else could we live in the present knowing it was the present except in the context of the important things that have already happened? No, one must treasure each moment of the past, get the same thrill from it that one gets from watching each moment of an old movie. These windows on the past enable us to see enough to stay on an even keel in the razor's-edge present which is really a no-time, continually straying over the border into the positive past and the negative future whose movements alone define it. Unfortunately we have to live in it. We are appalled at this. Because its no-time, no-space dimensions offer us no signposts, nothing to be guided by. In this dimensionless area a single step can be leagues or inches; the flame of a match can seem like an explosion on the sun or it can make no dent in the matte-gray, uniform night. The jolting and loss of gravity produce a permanent condition of nausea, always buzzing faintly at the blurred edge where life is hinged to the future and to the past. But only focus on the past through the clear movie-theater dark and you are a changed person, and can begin to live again. That is why we, snatched from sudden freedom, are able to communicate only through this celluloid vehicle that has immortalized and given a definitive shape to our formless gestures; we can live as though we had caught up with time and avoid the sickness of the present, a shapeless blur as meaningless as a carelessly exposed roll of film. There is hardness and density now, and our story takes on the clear, compact shape of the plot of a novel, with all its edges and inner passages laid bare for the reader, to be resumed and resumed over and over, that is taken up and put aside and taken up again.

What place is there in the continuing story for all the adventures, the wayward pleasures, the medium-size experiences that somehow don't fit in but which loom larger and more interesting as they begin to retreat into the past? There were so many things held back, kept back, because they didn't fit into the plot or because their tone wasn't in keeping with the whole. So many of these things have been discarded, and they now tower on the brink of the continuity, hemming it in like dark crags above a valley stream. One sometimes forgets that to be all one way may be preferable to eclectic diversity in the interests of verisimilitude, even for those of the opposite persuasion; the most powerful preachers are those persuaded in advance and their unalterable lessons are deeply moving just because of this rigidity, having none of the tepidness of the meandering stream of our narration with its well-chosen and typical episodes, which now seems to be trying to bury itself in the landscape. The rejected chapters have taken over. For a long time it was as though only the most patient scholar or the recording angel himself would ever interest himself in them. Now it seems as though that angel had begun to dominate the whole story: he who was supposed only to copy it all down has joined forces with the misshapen, misfit pieces that were never meant to go into it but at best to stay on the sidelines so as to point up how everything else belonged together, and the resulting mountain of data threatens us; one can almost hear the beginning of the lyric crash in which everything will be lost and pulverized, changed back into atoms ready to resume new combinations and shapes again, new wilder tendencies, as foreign to what we have carefully put in and kept out as a new chart of elements or another planet—unimaginable, in a word. And would you believe that this word could possibly be our salvation? For we are rescued by what we cannot imagine: it is what finally takes us up and shuts our story, replacing it among the millions of similar volumes that by no means menace its uniqueness but on the contrary situate it in the proper depth and perspective. At last we have that rightness that is rightfully ours. But we do not know what brought it about.

It could be anything, you say. But it could not have been an exercise in defining the present when our position, our very lives depend on those fixed loci of past and future that leave no room for the nominal existence of anything else. But it turns out you have been pursuing the discussion in a leisurely way throughout January and February and now to a point farther into the wilderness of this new year which makes such a commotion and goes by so quickly. These ample digressions of yours have carried you ahead to a distant and seemingly remote place, and it is here that you stop to give emphasis to all the way you have traveled and to your present silence. And it is here that I am quite ready to admit that I am alone, that the film I have been watching all this time may be only a mirror, with all the characters including that of the old aunt played by me in different disguises. If you need a certain vitality you can only supply it yourself, or there comes a point, anyway, when no one's actions but your own seem dramatically convincing and justifiable in the plot that the number of your days concocts. I have been watching this film, therefore, and now I have seen enough; as I leave the theater I am surprised to find that it is still daylight outside (the darkness of the film as well as its specks of light were so intense); I am forced to squint; in this way I gradually get an idea of where I am. Only this world is not as light as the other one; it is made gray with shadows like cobwebs that deepen as the memory of the film begins to fade. This is the way all movies are meant to end, but how is it possible to go on living just now except by plunging into the middle of some other one that you have doubtless seen before? It seems truly impossible, but invariably at this point we are walking together along a street in some well-known city. The allegory is ended, its coils absorbed into the past, and this afternoon is as wide as an ocean. It is the time we have now, and all our wasted time sinks into the sea and is swallowed up without a trace. The past is dust and ashes, and this incommensurably wide way leads to the pragmatic and kinetic future.

From
SELF-
PORTRAIT
IN A
CONVEX
MIRROR

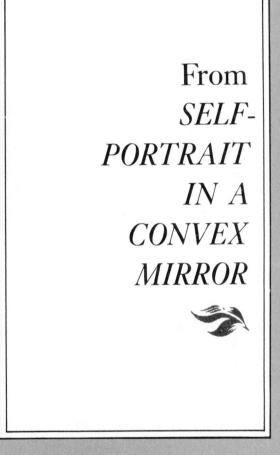

AS ONE PUT DRUNK
INTO THE PACKET-BOAT

I tried each thing, only some were immortal and free.
Elsewhere we are as sitting in a place where sunlight
Filters down, a little at a time,
Waiting for someone to come. Harsh words are spoken,
As the sun yellows the green of the maple tree. . . .

So this was all, but obscurely
I felt the stirrings of new breath in the pages
Which all winter long had smelled like an old catalogue.
New sentences were starting up. But the summer
Was well along, not yet past the mid-point
But full and dark with the promise of that fullness,
That time when one can no longer wander away
And even the least attentive fall silent
To watch the thing that is prepared to happen.

A look of glass stops you
And you walk on shaken: was I the perceived?
Did they notice me, this time, as I am,
Or is it postponed again? The children
Still at their games, clouds that arise with a swift
Impatience in the afternoon sky, then dissipate
As limpid, dense twilight comes.
Only in that tooting of a horn
Down there, for a moment, I thought
The great, formal affair was beginning, orchestrated,
Its colors concentrated in a glance, a ballade
That takes in the whole world, now, but lightly,
Still lightly, but with wide authority and tact.

The prevalence of those gray flakes falling?
They are sun motes. You have slept in the sun
Longer than the sphinx, and are none the wiser for it.
Come in. And I thought a shadow fell across the door

But it was only her come to ask once more
If I was coming in, and not to hurry in case I wasn't.

The night sheen takes over. A moon of cistercian pallor
Has climbed to the center of heaven, installed,
Finally involved with the business of darkness.
And a sigh heaves from all the small things on earth,
The books, the papers, the old garters and union-suit buttons
Kept in a white cardboard box somewhere, and all the lower
Versions of cities flattened under the equalizing night.
The summer demands and takes away too much,
But night, the reserved, the reticent, gives more than it takes.

WORSENING SITUATION

Like a rainstorm, he said, the braided colors
Wash over me and are no help. Or like one
At a feast who eats not, for he cannot choose
From among the smoking dishes. This severed hand
Stands for life, and wander as it will,
East or west, north or south, it is ever
A stranger who walks beside me. O seasons,
Booths, chaleur, dark-hatted charlatans
On the outskirts of some rural fete,
The name you drop and never say is mine, mine!
Some day I'll claim to you how all used up
I am because of you but in the meantime the ride
Continues. Everyone is along for the ride,
It seems. Besides, what else is there?
The annual games? True, there are occasions
For white uniforms and a special language
Kept secret from the others. The limes
Are duly sliced. I know all this
But can't seem to keep it from affecting me,
Every day, all day. I've tried recreation,
Reading until late at night, train rides
And romance.
                    One day a man called while I was out
And left this message: "You got the whole thing wrong
From start to finish. Luckily, there's still time
To correct the situation, but you must act fast.
See me at your earliest convenience. And please,
Tell no one of this. Much besides your life depends on it."
I thought nothing of it at the time. Lately
I've been looking at old-fashioned plaids, fingering
Starched white collars, wondering whether there's a way
To get them really white again. My wife
Thinks I'm in Oslo—Oslo, France, that is.

FORTIES FLICK

The shadow of the Venetian blind on the painted wall,
Shadows of the snake-plant and cacti, the plaster animals,
Focus the tragic melancholy of the bright stare
Into nowhere, a hole like the black holes in space.
In bra and panties she sidles to the window:
Zip! Up with the blind. A fragile street scene offers itself,
With wafer-thin pedestrians who know where they are going.
The blind comes down slowly, the slats are slowly tilted up.

Why must it always end this way?
A dais with woman reading, with the ruckus of her hair
And all that is unsaid about her pulling us back to her, with her
Into the silence that night alone can't explain.
Silence of the library, of the telephone with its pad,
But we didn't have to reinvent these either:
They had gone away into the plot of a story,
The "art" part—knowing what important details to leave out
And the way character is developed. Things too real
To be of much concern, hence artificial, yet now all over the page,
The indoors with the outside becoming part of you
As you find you had never left off laughing at death,
The background, dark vine at the edge of the porch.

AS YOU CAME FROM
THE HOLY LAND

of western New York state
were the graves all right in their bushings
was there a note of panic in the late August air
because the old man had peed in his pants again
was there turning away from the late afternoon glare
as though it too could be wished away
was any of this present
and how could this be
the magic solution to what you are in now
whatever has held you motionless
like this so long through the dark season
until now the women come out in navy blue
and the worms come out of the compost to die
it is the end of any season

you reading there so accurately
sitting not wanting to be disturbed
as you came from that holy land
what other signs of earth's dependency were upon you
what fixed sign at the crossroads
what lethargy in the avenues
where all is said in a whisper
what tone of voice among the hedges
what tone under the apple trees
the numbered land stretches away
and your house is built in tomorrow
but surely not before the examination
of what is right and will befall
not before the census
and the writing down of names

remember you are free to wander away
as from other times other scenes that were taking place
the history of someone who came too late

the time is ripe now and the adage
is hatching as the seasons change and tremble
it is finally as though that thing of monstrous interest
were happening in the sky
but the sun is setting and prevents you from seeing it

out of night the token emerges
its leaves like birds alighting all at once under a tree
taken up and shaken again
put down in weak rage
knowing as the brain does it can never come about
not here not yesterday in the past
only in the gap of today filling itself
as emptiness is distributed
in the idea of what time it is
when that time is already past

SCHEHERAZADE

Unsupported by reason's enigma
Water collects in squared stone catch basins.
The land is dry. Under it moves
The water. Fish live in the wells. The leaves,
A concerned green, are scrawled on the light. Bad
Bindweed and rank ragweed somehow forget to flourish here.
An inexhaustible wardrobe has been placed at the disposal
Of each new occurrence. It can be itself now.
Day is almost reluctant to decline
And slowing down opens out new avenues
That don't infringe on space but are living here with us.
Other dreams came and left while the bank
Of colored verbs and adjectives was shrinking from the light
To nurse in shade their want of a method
But most of all she loved the particles
That transform objects of the same category
Into particular ones, each distinct
Within and apart from its own class.
In all this springing up was no hint
Of a tide, only a pleasant wavering of the air
In which all things seemed present, whether
Just past or soon to come. It was all invitation.
So much the flowers outlined along the night
Alleys when few were visible, yet
Their story sounded louder than the hum
Of bug and stick noises that brought up the rear,
Trundling it along into a new fact of day.
These were meant to be read as any
Salutation before getting down to business,
But they stuck to their guns, and so much
Was their obstinacy in keeping with the rest
(Like long flashes of white birds that refuse to die
When day does) that none knew the warp

Which presented this major movement as a firm
Digression, a plain that slowly becomes a mountain.

So each found himself caught in a net
As a fashion, and all efforts to wriggle free
Involved him further, inexorably, since all
Existed there to be told, shot through
From border to border. Here were stones
That read as patches of sunlight, there was the story
Of the grandparents, of the vigorous young champion
(The lines once given to another, now
Restored to the new speaker), dinners and assemblies,
The light in the old home, the secret way
The rooms fed into each other, but all
Was wariness of time watching itself
For nothing in the complex story grew outside:
The greatness in the moment of telling stayed unresolved
Until its wealth of incident, pain mixed with pleasure,
Faded in the precise moment of bursting
Into bloom, its growth a static lament.

Some stories survived the dynasty of the builders
But their echo was itself locked in, became
Anticipation that was only memory after all,
For the possibilities are limited. It is seen
At the end that the kind and good are rewarded,
That the unjust one is doomed to burn forever
Around his error, sadder and wiser anyway.
Between these extremes the others muddle through
Like us, uncertain but wearing artlessly
Their function of minor characters who must
Be kept in mind. It is we who make this
Jungle and call it space, naming each root,
Each serpent, for the sound of the name

As it clinks dully against our pleasure,
Indifference that is pleasure. And what would they be
Without an audience to restrict the innumerable
Passes and swipes, restored to good humor as it issues
Into the impervious evening air? So in some way
Although the arithmetic is incorrect
The balance is restored because it
Balances, knowing it prevails,
And the man who made the same mistake twice is exonerated.

GRAND GALOP

All things seem mention of themselves
And the names which stem from them branch out to other
  referents.
Hugely, spring exists again. The weigela does its dusty thing
In fire-hammered air. And garbage cans are heaved against
The railing as the tulips yawn and crack open and fall apart.
And today is Monday. Today's lunch is: Spanish omelet, lettuce and
  tomato salad,
Jello, milk and cookies. Tomorrow's: sloppy joe on bun,
Scalloped corn, stewed tomatoes, rice pudding and milk.
The names we stole don't remove us:
We have moved on a little ahead of them
And now it is time to wait again.
Only waiting, the waiting: what fills up the time between?
It is another kind of wait, waiting for the wait to be ended.
Nothing takes up its fair share of time,
The wait is built into the things just coming into their own.
Nothing is partially incomplete, but the wait
Invests everything like a climate.
What time of day is it?
Does anything matter?
Yes, for you must wait to see what it is really like,
This event rounding the corner
Which will be unlike anything else and really
Cause no surprise: it's too ample.

Water
Drops from an air conditioner
On those who pass underneath. It's one of the sights of our town.
Puaagh. Vomit. Puaaaaagh. More vomit. One who comes
Walking dog on leash is distant to say how all this
Changes the minute to an hour, the hour
To the times of day, days to months, those easy-to-grasp entities,
And the months to seasons, which are far other, foreign

To our concept of time. Better the months—
They are almost persons—than these abstractions
That sift like marble dust across the unfinished works of the studio
Aging everything into a characterization of itself.
Better the cleanup committee concern itself with
Some item that is now little more than a feature
Of some obsolete style—cornice or spandrel
Out of the dimly remembered whole
Which probably lacks true distinction. But if one may pick it up,
Carry it over there, set it down,
Then the work is redeemed at the end
Under the smiling expanse of the sky
That plays no favorites but in the same way
Is honor only to those who have sought it.

The dog barks, the caravan passes on.
The words had a sort of bloom on them
But were weightless, carrying past what was being said.
"A nice time," you think, "to go out:
The early night is cool, but not
Too anything. People parading with their pets
Past lawns and vacant lots, as though these too were somehow
    imponderables
Before going home to the decency of one's private life
Shut up behind doors, which is nobody's business.
It does matter a little to the others
But only because it makes them realize how far their respect
Has brought them. No one would dare to intrude.
It is a night like many another
With the sky now a bit impatient for today to be over
Like a bored salesgirl shifting from foot to stockinged foot."
These khaki undershorts hung out on lines,
The wind billowing among them, are we never to make a statement?
And certain buildings we always pass which are never mentioned—

It's getting out of hand.
As long as one has some sense that each thing knows its place
All is well, but with the arrival and departure
Of each new one overlapping so intensely in the semi-darkness
It's a bit mad. Too bad, I mean, that getting to know each just for a
    fleeting second
Must be replaced by imperfect knowledge of the featureless whole,
Like some pocket history of the world, so general
As to constitute a sob or wail unrelated
To any attempt at definition. And the minor eras
Take on an importance out of all proportion to the story
For it can no longer unwind, but must be kept on hand
Indefinitely, like a first-aid kit no one ever uses
Or a word in the dictionary that no one will ever look up.
The custard is setting; meanwhile
I not only have my own history to worry about
But am forced to fret over insufficient details related to large
Unfinished concepts that can never bring themselves to the point
Of being, with or without my help, if any were forthcoming.

It is just the movement of the caravan away
Into an abstract night, with no
Precise goal in view, and indeed not caring,
That distributes this pause. Why be in a hurry
To speed away in the opposite direction, toward the other end of infinity?
For things can harden meaningfully in the moment of indecision.
I cannot decide in which direction to walk
But this doesn't matter to me, and I might as well
Decide to climb a mountain (it looks almost flat)
As decide to go home
Or to a bar or restaurant or to the home
Of some friend as charming and ineffectual as I am
Because these pauses are supposed to be life
And they sink steel needles deep into the pores, as though to say

There is no use trying to escape
And it is all here anyway. And their steep, slippery sides defy
Any notion of continuity. It is this
That takes us back into what really is, it seems, history—
The lackluster, disorganized kind without dates
That speaks out of the hollow trunk of a tree
To warn away the merely polite, or those whose destiny
Leaves them no time to quibble about the means,
Which are not ends, and yet . . . What precisely is it
About the time of day it is, the weather, that causes people to note it
    painstakingly in their diaries
For them to read who shall come after?
Surely it is because the ray of light
Or gloom striking you this moment is hope
In all its mature, matronly form, taking all things into account
And reapportioning them according to size
So that if one can't say that this is the natural way
It should have happened, at least one can have no cause for complaint
Which is the same as having reached the end, wise
In that expectation and enhanced by its fulfillment, or the absence of it.
But we say, it cannot come to any such end
As long as we are left around with no place to go.
And yet it has ended, and the thing we have fulfilled we have become.

Now it is the impulse of morning that makes
My watch tick. As one who pokes his head
Out from under a pile of blankets, the good and bad together,
So this tangle of impossible resolutions and irresolutions:
The desire to have fun, to make noise, and so to
Add to the already all-but-illegible scrub forest of graffiti on the shithouse
    wall.
Someone is coming to get you:
The mailman, or a butler enters with a letter on a tray
Whose message is to change everything, but in the meantime

One is to worry about one's smell or dandruff or lost glasses—
If only the curtain-raiser would end, but it is interminable.
But there is this consolation:
If it turns out to be not worth doing, I haven't done it;
If the sight appalls me, I have seen nothing;
If the victory is pyrrhic, I haven't won it.
And so from a day replete with rumors
Of things being done on the other side of the mountains
A nucleus remains, a still-perfect possibility
That can be kept indefinitely. And yet
The groans of labor pains are deafening; one must
Get up, get out and be on with it. Morning is for sissies like you
But the real trials, the ones that separate the men from the boys, come
    later.

Oregon was kinder to us. The streets
Offered a variety of directions to the foot
And bookstores where pornography is sold. But then
One whiffs just a slight odor of madness in the air.
They all got into their cars and drove away
As in the end of a movie. So that it finally made no difference
Whether this were the end or it was somewhere else:
If it had to be somewhere it might as well be
Here, on top of one. Here, as elsewhere,
April advances new suggestions, and one may as well
Move along with them, especially in view of
The midnight-blue light that in turning itself inside out
Offers something strange to the attention, a thing
That is not itself, gnat whirling before my eyes
At an incredible, tame velocity. Too pronounced after all
To be that meaningless. And so on to afternoon
On the desert, with oneself cleaned up, and the location
Almost brand-new what with the removal of gum wrappers, etc.
But I was trying to tell you about a strange thing

That happened to me, but this is no way to tell about it,
By making it truly happen. It drifts away in fragments.
And one is left sitting in the yard
To try to write poetry
Using what Wyatt and Surrey left around,
Took up and put down again
Like so much gorgeous raw material,
As though it would always happen in some way
And meanwhile since we are all advancing
It is sure to come about in spite of everything
On a Sunday, where you are left sitting
In the shade that, as always, is just a little too cool.
So there is whirling out at you from the not deep
Emptiness the word "cock" or some other, brother and sister words
With not much to be expected from them, though these
Are the ones that waited so long for you and finally left, having given up
   hope.
There is a note of desperation in one's voice, pleading for them,
And meanwhile the intensity thins and sharpens
Its point, that is the thing it was going to ask.
One has been waiting around all evening for it
Before sleep had stopped definitively the eyes and ears
Of all those who came as an audience.
Still, that poetry does sometimes occur
If only in creases in forgotten letters
Packed away in trunks in the attic—things you forgot you had
And what would it matter anyway,
That recompense so precisely dosed
As to seem the falling true of a perverse judgment.
You forget how there could be a gasp of a new air
Hidden in that jumble. And of course your forgetting
Is a sign of just how much it matters to you:
"It must have been important."
The lies fall like flaxen threads from the skies

All over America, and the fact that some of them are true of course
Doesn't so much not matter as serve to justify
The whole mad organizing force under the billows of correct delight.
Surrey, your lute is getting an attack of nervous paralysis
But there are, again, things to be sung of
And this is one of them, only I would not dream of intruding on
The frantic completeness, the all-purpose benevolence
Of that still-moist garden where the tooting originates:
Between intervals of clenched teeth, your venomous rondelay.

Ask a hog what is happening. Go on. Ask him.
The road just seems to vanish
And not that far in the distance, either. The horizon must have been
    moved up.
So it is that by limping carefully
From one day to the next, one approaches a worn, round stone tower
Crouching low in the hollow of a gully
With no door or window but a lot of old license plates
Tacked up over a slit too narrow for a wrist to pass through
And a sign: "Van Camp's Pork and Beans."
From then on in: *angst*-colored skies, emotional withdrawals
As the whole business starts to frighten even you,
Its originator and promoter. The horizon returns
As a smile of recognition this time, polite, unquestioning.
How long ago high school graduation seems
Yet it cannot have been so very long:
One has traveled such a short distance.
The styles haven't changed much,
And I still have a sweater and one or two other things I had then.
It seems only yesterday that we saw
The movie with the cows in it
And turned to one at your side, who burped
As morning saw a new garnet-and-pea-green order propose
Itself out of the endless bathos, like science-fiction lumps.

Impossible not to be moved by the tiny number
Those people wore, indicating they should be raised to this or
    that power.
But now we are at Cape Fear and the overland trail
Is impassable, and a dense curtain of mist hangs over the sea.

HOP O' MY THUMB

The grand hotels, dancing girls
Urge forward under a veil of "lost illusion"
The deed to this day or some other day.
There is no day in the calendar
The dairy company sent out
That lets you possess it wildly like
The body of a dreaming woman in a dream:
All flop over at the top when seized,
The stem too slender, the top too loose and heavy,
Blushing with fine foliage of dreams.
The motor cars, tinsel hats,
Supper of cakes, the amorous children
Take the solitary downward path of dreams
And are not seen again.
What is it, Undine?
The notes now can scarcely be heard
In the hubbub of the flattening storm,
With the third wish unspoken.

I remember meeting you in a dark dream
Of April, you or some girl,
The necklace of wishes alive and breathing around your throat.
In the blindness of that dark whose
Brightness turned to sand salt-glazed in noon sun
We could not know each other or know which part
Belonged to the other, pelted in an electric storm of rain.
Only gradually the mounds that meant our bodies
That wore our selves concaved into view
But intermittently as through dark mist
Smeared against fog. No worse time to have come,
Yet all was desiring though already desired and past,
The moment a monument to itself
No one would ever see or know was there.

That time faded too and the night
Softened to smooth spirals or foliage at night.
There were sleeping cabins near by, blind lanterns,
Nocturnal friendliness of the plate of milk left for the fairies
Who otherwise might be less well disposed:
Friendship of white sheets patched with milk.
And always an open darkness in which one name
Cries over and over again: Ariane! Ariane!
Was it for this you led your sisters back from sleep
And now he of the blue beard has outmaneuvered you?
But for the best perhaps: let
Those sisters slink into the sapphire
Hair that is mounting day.
There are still other made-up countries
Where we can hide forever,
Wasted with eternal desire and sadness,
Sucking the sherbets, crooning the tunes, naming the names.

MIXED FEELINGS

A pleasant smell of frying sausages
Attacks the sense, along with an old, mostly invisible
Photograph of what seems to be girls lounging around
An old fighter bomber, circa 1942 vintage.
How to explain to these girls, if indeed that's what they are,
These Ruths, Lindas, Pats and Sheilas
About the vast change that's taken place
In the fabric of our society, altering the texture
Of all things in it? And yet
They somehow look as if they knew, except
That it's so hard to see them, it's hard to figure out
Exactly what kind of expressions they're wearing.
What are your hobbies, girls? Aw nerts,
One of them might say, this guy's too much for me.
Let's go on and out, somewhere
Through the canyons of the garment center
To a small café and have a cup of coffee.
I am not offended that these creatures (that's the word)
Of my imagination seem to hold me in such light esteem,
Pay so little heed to me. It's part of a complicated
Flirtation routine, anyhow, no doubt. But this talk of
The garment center? Surely that's California sunlight
Belaboring them and the old crate on which they
Have draped themselves, fading its Donald Duck insignia
To the extreme point of legibility.
Maybe they were lying but more likely their
Tiny intelligences cannot retain much information.
Not even one fact, perhaps. That's why
They think they're in New York. I like the way
They look and act and feel. I wonder
How they got that way, but am not going to
Waste any more time thinking about them.
I have already forgotten them
Until some day in the not too distant future

When we meet possibly in the lounge of a modern airport,
They looking as astonishingly young and fresh as when this picture was
  made
But full of contradictory ideas, stupid ones as well as
Worthwhile ones, but all flooding the surface of our minds
As we babble about the sky and the weather and the forests of change.

MÄRCHENBILDER

Es war einmal . . . No, it's too heavy
To be said. Besides, you aren't paying attention any more.
How shall I put it?
"The rain thundered on the uneven red flagstones.

The steadfast tin soldier gazed beyond the drops
Remembering the hat-shaped paper boat, that soon . . ."
That's not it either.
Think about the long summer evenings of the past, the queen anne's lace.

Sometimes a musical phrase would perfectly sum up
The mood of a moment. One of those lovelorn sonatas
For wind instruments was riding past on a solemn white horse.
Everybody wondered who the new arrival was.

Pomp of flowers, decorations
Junked next day. Now look out of the window.
The sky is clear and bland. The wrong kind of day
For business or games, or betting on a sure thing.

The trees weep drops
Into the water at night. Slowly couples gather.
She looks into his eyes. "It would not be good
To be left alone." He: "I'll stay

As long as the night allows." This was one of those night rainbows
In negative color. As we advance, it retreats; we see
We are now far into a cave, must be. Yet there seem to be
Trees all around, and a wind lifts their leaves, slightly.

I want to go back, out of the bad stories,
But there's always the possibility that the next one . . .
No, it's another almond tree, or a ring-swallowing frog . . .
Yet they are beautiful as we people them

With ourselves. They are empty as cupboards.
To spend whole days drenched in them, waiting for the next whisper,
For the word in the next room. This is how the princes must have
  behaved,
Lying down in the frugality of sleep.

OLEUM MISERICORDIAE

To rub it out, make it less virulent
And a stab too at rearranging
The whole thing from the ground up.
Yes we were waiting just now
Yes we are no longer waiting.

Afterwards when I tell you
It's as though it all only happened
As siding of my story

I beg you to listen
You are already listening

It has shut itself out
And in doing so shut us accidentally in

And meanwhile my story goes well
The first chapter
                endeth

But the real story, the one
They tell us we shall probably never know
Drifts back in bits and pieces
All of them, it turns out

So lucky
Now we really know
It all happened by chance:
A chance encounter
The dwarf led you to the end of a street
And pointed flapping his arms in two directions
You forgot to misprize him
But after a series of interludes
In furnished rooms (describe wallpaper)

Transient hotels (mention sink and cockroaches)
And spending the night with a beautiful married woman
Whose husband was away in Centerville on business
(Mention this wallpaper: the purest roses
Though the creamiest and how
Her smile lightens the ordeal
Of the last 500 pages
Though you never knew her last name
Only her first: Dorothy)
You got hold of the water of life
Rescued your two wicked brothers Cash and Jethro
Who promptly stole the water of life
After which you got it back, got safely home,
Saved the old man's life
And inherited the kingdom.

But this was a moment
Under the most cheerful sun.
In poorer lands
No one touches the water of life.

It has no taste
And though it refreshes absolutely
It is a cup that must also pass

Until everybody
Gets some advantage, big or little
Some reason for having come
So far
Without dog or woman
So far alone, unasked.

SELF-PORTRAIT
IN A CONVEX MIRROR

As Parmigianino did it, the right hand
Bigger than the head, thrust at the viewer
And swerving easily away, as though to protect
What it advertises. A few leaded panes, old beams,
Fur, pleated muslin, a coral ring run together
In a movement supporting the face, which swims
Toward and away like the hand
Except that it is in repose. It is what is
Sequestered. Vasari says, "Francesco one day set himself
To take his own portrait, looking at himself for that purpose
In a convex mirror, such as is used by barbers . . .
He accordingly caused a ball of wood to be made
By a turner, and having divided it in half and
Brought it to the size of the mirror, he set himself
With great art to copy all that he saw in the glass,"
Chiefly his reflection, of which the portrait
Is the reflection once removed.
The glass chose to reflect only what he saw
Which was enough for his purpose: his image
Glazed, embalmed, projected at a 180-degree angle.
The time of day or the density of the light
Adhering to the face keeps it
Lively and intact in a recurring wave
Of arrival. The soul establishes itself.
But how far can it swim out through the eyes
And still return safely to its nest? The surface
Of the mirror being convex, the distance increases
Significantly; that is, enough to make the point
That the soul is a captive, treated humanely, kept
In suspension, unable to advance much farther
Than your look as it intercepts the picture.
Pope Clement and his court were "stupefied"
By it, according to Vasari, and promised a commission
That never materialized. The soul has to stay where it is,

Even though restless, hearing raindrops at the pane,
The sighing of autumn leaves thrashed by the wind,
Longing to be free, outside, but it must stay
Posing in this place. It must move
As little as possible. This is what the portrait says.
But there is in that gaze a combination
Of tenderness, amusement and regret, so powerful
In its restraint that one cannot look for long.
The secret is too plain. The pity of it smarts,
Makes hot tears spurt: that the soul is not a soul,
Has no secret, is small, and it fits
Its hollow perfectly: its room, our moment of attention.
That is the tune but there are no words.
The words are only speculation
(From the Latin *speculum*, mirror):
They seek and cannot find the meaning of the music.
We see only postures of the dream,
Riders of the motion that swings the face
Into view under evening skies, with no
False disarray as proof of authenticity.
But it is life englobed.
One would like to stick one's hand
Out of the globe, but its dimension,
What carries it, will not allow it.
No doubt it is this, not the reflex
To hide something, which makes the hand loom large
As it retreats slightly. There is no way
To build it flat like a section of wall:
It must join the segment of a circle,
Roving back to the body of which it seems
So unlikely a part, to fence in and shore up the face
On which the effort of this condition reads
Like a pinpoint of a smile, a spark
Or star one is not sure of having seen

As darkness resumes. A perverse light whose
Imperative of subtlety dooms in advance its
Conceit to light up: unimportant but meant.
Francesco, your hand is big enough
To wreck the sphere, and too big,
One would think, to weave delicate meshes
That only argue its further detention.
(Big, but not coarse, merely on another scale,
Like a dozing whale on the sea bottom
In relation to the tiny, self-important ship
On the surface.) But your eyes proclaim
That everything is surface. The surface is what's there
And nothing can exist except what's there.
There are no recesses in the room, only alcoves,
And the window doesn't matter much, or that
Sliver of window or mirror on the right, even
As a gauge of the weather, which in French is
Le temps, the word for time, and which
Follows a course wherein changes are merely
Features of the whole. The whole is stable within
Instability, a globe like ours, resting
On a pedestal of vacuum, a ping-pong ball
Secure on its jet of water.
And just as there are no words for the surface, that is,
No words to say what it really is, that it is not
Superficial but a visible core, then there is
No way out of the problem of pathos vs. experience.
You will stay on, restive, serene in
Your gesture which is neither embrace nor warning
But which holds something of both in pure
Affirmation that doesn't affirm anything.

The balloon pops, the attention
Turns dully away. Clouds

In the puddle stir up into sawtoothed fragments.
I think of the friends
Who came to see me, of what yesterday
Was like. A peculiar slant
Of memory that intrudes on the dreaming model
In the silence of the studio as he considers
Lifting the pencil to the self-portrait.
How many people came and stayed a certain time,
Uttered light or dark speech that became part of you
Like light behind windblown fog and sand,
Filtered and influenced by it, until no part
Remains that is surely you. Those voices in the dusk
Have told you all and still the tale goes on
In the form of memories deposited in irregular
Clumps of crystals. Whose curved hand controls,
Francesco, the turning seasons and the thoughts
That peel off and fly away at breathless speeds
Like the last stubborn leaves ripped
From wet branches? I see in this only the chaos
Of your round mirror which organizes everything
Around the polestar of your eyes which are empty,
Know nothing, dream but reveal nothing.
I feel the carousel starting slowly
And going faster and faster: desk, papers, books,
Photographs of friends, the window and the trees
Merging in one neutral band that surrounds
Me on all sides, everywhere I look.
And I cannot explain the action of leveling,
Why it should all boil down to one
Uniform substance, a magma of interiors.
My guide in these matters is your self,
Firm, oblique, accepting everything with the same
Wraith of a smile, and as time speeds up so that it is soon
Much later, I can know only the straight way out,

The distance between us. Long ago
The strewn evidence meant something,
The small accidents and pleasures
Of the day as it moved gracelessly on,
A housewife doing chores. Impossible now
To restore those properties in the silver blur that is
The record of what you accomplished by sitting down
"With great art to copy all that you saw in the glass"
So as to perfect and rule out the extraneous
Forever. In the circle of your intentions certain spars
Remain that perpetuate the enchantment of self with self:
Eyebeams, muslin, coral. It doesn't matter
Because these are things as they are today
Before one's shadow ever grew
Out of the field into thoughts of tomorrow.

Tomorrow is easy, but today is uncharted,
Desolate, reluctant as any landscape
To yield what are laws of perspective
After all only to the painter's deep
Mistrust, a weak instrument though
Necessary. Of course some things
Are possible, it knows, but it doesn't know
Which ones. Some day we will try
To do as many things as are possible
And perhaps we shall succeed at a handful
Of them, but this will not have anything
To do with what is promised today, our
Landscape sweeping out from us to disappear
On the horizon. Today enough of a cover burnishes
To keep the supposition of promises together
In one piece of surface, letting one ramble
Back home from them so that these
Even stronger possibilities can remain

Whole without being tested. Actually
The skin of the bubble-chamber's as tough as
Reptile eggs; everything gets "programmed" there
In due course: more keeps getting included
Without adding to the sum, and just as one
Gets accustomed to a noise that
Kept one awake but now no longer does,
So the room contains this flow like an hourglass
Without varying in climate or quality
(Except perhaps to brighten bleakly and almost
Invisibly, in a focus of sharpening toward death—more
Of this later). What should be the vacuum of a dream
Becomes continually replete as the source of dreams
Is being tapped so that this one dream
May wax, flourish like a cabbage rose,
Defying sumptuary laws, leaving us
To awake and try to begin living in what
Has now become a slum. Sydney Freedberg in his
Parmigianino says of it: "Realism in this portrait
No longer produces an objective truth, but a *bizarria*. . . .
However its distortion does not create
A feeling of disharmony. . . . The forms retain
A strong measure of ideal beauty," because
Fed by our dreams, so inconsequential until one day
We notice the hole they left. Now their importance
If not their meaning is plain. They were to nourish
A dream which includes them all, as they are
Finally reversed in the accumulating mirror.
They seemed strange because we couldn't actually see them.
And we realize this only at a point where they lapse
Like a wave breaking on a rock, giving up
Its shape in a gesture which expresses that shape.
The forms retain a strong measure of ideal beauty
As they forage in secret on our idea of distortion.

Why be unhappy with this arrangement, since
Dreams prolong us as they are absorbed?
Something like living occurs, a movement
Out of the dream into its codification.

As I start to forget it
It presents its stereotype again
But it is an unfamiliar stereotype, the face
Riding at anchor, issued from hazards, soon
To accost others, "rather angel than man" (Vasari).
Perhaps an angel looks like everything
We have forgotten, I mean forgotten
Things that don't seem familiar when
We meet them again, lost beyond telling
Which were ours once. This would be the point
Of invading the privacy of this man who
"Dabbled in alchemy, but whose wish
Here was not to examine the subtleties of art
In a detached, scientific spirit: he wished through them
To impart the sense of novelty and amazement to the spectator"
(Freedberg). Later portraits such as the Uffizi
"Gentleman," the Borghese "Young Prelate" and
The Naples "Antea" issue from Mannerist
Tensions, but here, as Freedberg points out,
The surprise, the tension are in the concept
Rather than its realization.
The consonance of the High Renaissance
Is present, though distorted by the mirror.
What is novel is the extreme care in rendering
The velleities of the rounded reflecting surface
(It is the first mirror portrait),
So that you could be fooled for a moment
Before you realize the reflection
Isn't yours. You feel then like one of those

Hoffmann characters who have been deprived
Of a reflection, except that the whole of me
Is seen to be supplanted by the strict
Otherness of the painter in his
Other room. We have surprised him
At work, but no, he has surprised us
As he works. The picture is almost finished,
The surprise almost over, as when one looks out,
Startled by a snowfall which even now is
Ending in specks and sparkles of snow.
It happened while you were inside, asleep,
And there is no reason why you should have
Been awake for it, except that the day
Is ending and it will be hard for you
To get to sleep tonight, at least until late.

The shadow of the city injects its own
Urgency: Rome where Francesco
Was at work during the Sack: his inventions
Amazed the soldiers who burst in on him;
They decided to spare his life, but he left soon after;
Vienna where the painting is today, where
I saw it with Pierre in the summer of 1959; New York
Where I am now, which is a logarithm
Of other cities. Our landscape
Is alive with filiations, shuttlings;
Business is carried on by look, gesture,
Hearsay. It is another life to the city,
The backing of the looking glass of the
Unidentified but precisely sketched studio. It wants
To siphon off the life of the studio, deflate
Its mapped space to enactments, island it.
That operation has been temporarily stalled
But something new is on the way, a new preciosity

In the wind. Can you stand it,
Francesco? Are you strong enough for it?
This wind brings what it knows not, is
Self-propelled, blind, has no notion
Of itself. It is inertia that once
Acknowledged saps all activity, secret or public:
Whispers of the word that can't be understood
But can be felt, a chill, a blight
Moving outward along the capes and peninsulas
Of your nervures and so to the archipelagoes
And to the bathed, aired secrecy of the open sea.
This is its negative side. Its positive side is
Making you notice life and the stresses
That only seemed to go away, but now,
As this new mode questions, are seen to be
Hastening out of style. If they are to become classics
They must decide which side they are on.
Their reticence has undermined
The urban scenery, made its ambiguities
Look willful and tired, the games of an old man.
What we need now is this unlikely
Challenger pounding on the gates of an amazed
Castle. Your argument, Francesco,
Had begun to grow stale as no answer
Or answers were forthcoming. If it dissolves now
Into dust, that only means its time had come
Some time ago, but look now, and listen:
It may be that another life is stocked there
In recesses no one knew of; that it,
Not we, are the change; that we are in fact it
If we could get back to it, relive some of the way
It looked, turn our faces to the globe as it sets
And still be coming out all right:
Nerves normal, breath normal. Since it is a metaphor

Made to include us, we are a part of it and
Can live in it as in fact we have done,
Only leaving our minds bare for questioning
We now see will not take place at random
But in an orderly way that means to menace
Nobody—the normal way things are done,
Like the concentric growing up of days
Around a life: correctly, if you think about it.

A breeze like the turning of a page
Brings back your face: the moment
Takes such a big bite out of the haze
Of pleasant intuition it comes after.
The locking into place is "death itself,"
As Berg said of a phrase in Mahler's Ninth;
Or, to quote Imogen in *Cymbeline*, "There cannot
Be a pinch in death more sharp than this," for,
Though only exercise or tactic, it carries
The momentum of a conviction that had been building.
Mere forgetfulness cannot remove it
Nor wishing bring it back, as long as it remains
The white precipitate of its dream
In the climate of sighs flung across our world,
A cloth over a birdcage. But it is certain that
What is beautiful seems so only in relation to a specific
Life, experienced or not, channeled into some form
Steeped in the nostalgia of a collective past.
The light sinks today with an enthusiasm
I have known elsewhere, and known why
It seemed meaningful, that others felt this way
Years ago. I go on consulting
This mirror that is no longer mine
For as much brisk vacancy as is to be
My portion this time. And the vase is always full

Because there is only just so much room
And it accommodates everything. The sample
One sees is not to be taken as
Merely that, but as everything as it
May be imagined outside time—not as a gesture
But as all, in the refined, assimilable state.
But what is this universe the porch of
As it veers in and out, back and forth,
Refusing to surround us and still the only
Thing we can see? Love once
Tipped the scales but now is shadowed, invisible,
Though mysteriously present, around somewhere.
But we know it cannot be sandwiched
Between two adjacent moments, that its windings
Lead nowhere except to further tributaries
And that these empty themselves into a vague
Sense of something that can never be known
Even though it seems likely that each of us
Knows what it is and is capable of
Communicating it to the other. But the look
Some wear as a sign makes one want to
Push forward ignoring the apparent
Naïveté of the attempt, not caring
That no one is listening, since the light
Has been lit once and for all in their eyes
And is present, unimpaired, a permanent anomaly,
Awake and silent. On the surface of it
There seems no special reason why that light
Should be focused by love, or why
The city falling with its beautiful suburbs
Into space always less clear, less defined,
Should read as the support of its progress,
The easel upon which the drama unfolded
To its own satisfaction and to the end

Of our dreaming, as we had never imagined
It would end, in worn daylight with the painted
Promise showing through as a gage, a bond.
This nondescript, never-to-be defined daytime is
The secret of where it takes place
And we can no longer return to the various
Conflicting statements gathered, lapses of memory
Of the principal witnesses. All we know
Is that we are a little early, that
Today has that special, lapidary
Todayness that the sunlight reproduces
Faithfully in casting twig-shadows on blithe
Sidewalks. No previous day would have been like this.
I used to think they were all alike,
That the present always looked the same to everybody
But this confusion drains away as one
Is always cresting into one's present.
Yet the "poetic," straw-colored space
Of the long corridor that leads back to the painting,
Its darkening opposite—is this
Some figment of "art," not to be imagined
As real, let alone special? Hasn't it too its lair
In the present we are always escaping from
And falling back into, as the waterwheel of days
Pursues its uneventful, even serene course?
I think it is trying to say it is today
And we must get out of it even as the public
Is pushing through the museum now so as to
Be out by closing time. You can't live there.
The gray glaze of the past attacks all know-how:
Secrets of wash and finish that took a lifetime
To learn and are reduced to the status of
Black-and-white illustrations in a book where colorplates
Are rare. That is, all time

Reduces to no special time. No one
Alludes to the change; to do so might
Involve calling attention to oneself
Which would augment the dread of not getting out
Before having seen the whole collection
(Except for the sculptures in the basement:
They are where they belong).
Our time gets to be veiled, compromised
By the portrait's will to endure. It hints at
Our own, which we were hoping to keep hidden.
We don't need paintings or
Doggerel written by mature poets when
The explosion is so precise, so fine.
Is there any point even in acknowledging
The existence of all that? Does it
Exist? Certainly the leisure to
Indulge stately pastimes doesn't,
Any more. Today has no margins, the event arrives
Flush with its edges, is of the same substance,
Indistinguishable. "Play" is something else;
It exists, in a society specifically
Organized as a demonstration of itself.
There is no other way, and those assholes
Who would confuse everything with their mirror games
Which seem to multiply stakes and possibilities, or
At least confuse issues by means of an investing
Aura that would corrode the architecture
Of the whole in a haze of suppressed mockery,
Are beside the point. They are out of the game,
Which doesn't exist until they are out of it.
It seems like a very hostile universe
But as the principle of each individual thing is
Hostile to, exists at the expense of all the others
As philosophers have often pointed out, at least

This thing, the mute, undivided present,
Has the justification of logic, which
In this instance isn't a bad thing
Or wouldn't be, if the way of telling
Didn't somehow intrude, twisting the end result
Into a caricature of itself. This always
Happens, as in the game where
A whispered phrase passed around the room
Ends up as something completely different.
It is the principle that makes works of art so unlike
What the artist intended. Often he finds
He has omitted the thing he started out to say
In the first place. Seduced by flowers,
Explicit pleasures, he blames himself (though
Secretly satisfied with the result), imagining
He had a say in the matter and exercised
An option of which he was hardly conscious,
Unaware that necessity circumvents such resolutions
So as to create something new
For itself, that there is no other way,
That the history of creation proceeds according to
Stringent laws, and that things
Do get done in this way, but never the things
We set out to accomplish and wanted so desperately
To see come into being. Parmigianino
Must have realized this as he worked at his
Life-obstructing task. One is forced to read
The perfectly plausible accomplishment of a purpose
Into the smooth, perhaps even bland (but so
Enigmatic) finish. Is there anything
To be serious about beyond this otherness
That gets included in the most ordinary
Forms of daily activity, changing everything
Slightly and profoundly, and tearing the matter

Of creation, any creation, not just artistic creation
Out of our hands, to install it on some monstrous, near
Peak, too close to ignore, too far
For one to intervene? This otherness, this
"Not-being-us" is all there is to look at
In the mirror, though no one can say
How it came to be this way. A ship
Flying unknown colors has entered the harbor.
You are allowing extraneous matters
To break up your day, cloud the focus
Of the crystal ball. Its scene drifts away
Like vapor scattered on the wind. The fertile
Thought-associations that until now came
So easily, appear no more, or rarely. Their
Colorings are less intense, washed out
By autumn rains and winds, spoiled, muddied,
Given back to you because they are worthless.
Yet we are such creatures of habit that their
Implications are still around *en permanence*, confusing
Issues. To be serious only about sex
Is perhaps one way, but the sands are hissing
As they approach the beginning of the big slide
Into what happened. This past
Is now here: the painter's
Reflected face, in which we linger, receiving
Dreams and inspirations on an unassigned
Frequency, but the hues have turned metallic,
The curves and edges are not so rich. Each person
Has one big theory to explain the universe
But it doesn't tell the whole story
And in the end it is what is outside him
That matters, to him and especially to us
Who have been given no help whatever
In decoding our own man-size quotient and must rely

On second-hand knowledge. Yet I know
That no one else's taste is going to be
Any help, and might as well be ignored.
Once it seemed so perfect—gloss on the fine
Freckled skin, lips moistened as though about to part
Releasing speech, and the familiar look
Of clothes and furniture that one forgets.
This could have been our paradise: exotic
Refuge within an exhausted world, but that wasn't
In the cards, because it couldn't have been
The point. Aping naturalness may be the first step
Toward achieving an inner calm
But it is the first step only, and often
Remains a frozen gesture of welcome etched
On the air materializing behind it,
A convention. And we have really
No time for these, except to use them
For kindling. The sooner they are burnt up
The better for the roles we have to play.
Therefore I beseech you, withdraw that hand,
Offer it no longer as shield or greeting,
The shield of a greeting, Francesco:
There is room for one bullet in the chamber:
Our looking through the wrong end
Of the telescope as you fall back at a speed
Faster than that of light to flatten ultimately
Among the features of the room, an invitation
Never mailed, the "it was all a dream"
Syndrome, though the "all" tells tersely
Enough how it wasn't. Its existence
Was real, though troubled, and the ache
Of this waking dream can never drown out
The diagram still sketched on the wind,
Chosen, meant for me and materialized

In the disguising radiance of my room.
We have seen the city; it is the gibbous
Mirrored eye of an insect. All things happen
On its balcony and are resumed within,
But the action is the cold, syrupy flow
Of a pageant. One feels too confined,
Sifting the April sunlight for clues,
In the mere stillness of the ease of its
Parameter. The hand holds no chalk
And each part of the whole falls off
And cannot know it knew, except
Here and there, in cold pockets
Of remembrance, whispers out of time.

From
HOUSEBOAT DAYS

STREET MUSICIANS

One died, and the soul was wrenched out
Of the other in life, who, walking the streets
Wrapped in an identity like a coat, sees on and on
The same corners, volumetrics, shadows
Under trees. Farther than anyone was ever
Called, through increasingly suburban airs
And ways, with autumn falling over everything:
The plush leaves the chattels in barrels
Of an obscure family being evicted
Into the way it was, and is. The other beached
Glimpses of what the other was up to:
Revelations at last. So they grew to hate and forget each other.

So I cradle this average violin that knows
Only forgotten showtunes, but argues
The possibility of free declamation anchored
To a dull refrain, the year turning over on itself
In November, with the spaces among the days
More literal, the meat more visible on the bone.
Our question of a place of origin hangs
Like smoke: how we picnicked in pine forests,
In coves with the water always seeping up, and left
Our trash, sperm and excrement everywhere, smeared
On the landscape, to make of us what we could.

THE OTHER TRADITION

They all came, some wore sentiments
Emblazoned on T-shirts, proclaiming the lateness
Of the hour, and indeed the sun slanted its rays
Through branches of Norfolk Island pine as though
Politely clearing its throat, and all ideas settled
In a fuzz of dust under trees when it's drizzling:
The endless games of Scrabble, the boosters,
The celebrated omelette au Cantal, and through it
The roar of time plunging unchecked through the sluices
Of the days, dragging every sexual moment of it
Past the lenses: the end of something.
Only then did you glance up from your book,
Unable to comprehend what had been taking place, or
Say what you had been reading. More chairs
Were brought, and lamps were lit, but it tells
Nothing of how all this proceeded to materialize
Before you and the people waiting outside and in the next
Street, repeating its name over and over, until silence
Moved halfway up the darkened trunks,
And the meeting was called to order.

                                         I still remember
How they found you, after a dream, in your thimble hat,
Studious as a butterfly in a parking lot.
The road home was nicer then. Dispersing, each of the
Troubadours had something to say about how charity
Had run its race and won, leaving you the ex-president
Of the event, and how, though many of those present
Had wished something to come of it, if only a distant
Wisp of smoke, yet none was so deceived as to hanker
After that cool non-being of just a few minutes before,
Now that the idea of a forest had clamped itself
Over the minutiae of the scene. You found this
Charming, but turned your face fully toward night,

Speaking into it like a megaphone, not hearing
Or caring, although these still live and are generous
And all ways contained, allowed to come and go
Indefinitely in and out of the stockade
They have so much trouble remembering, when your forgetting
Rescues them at last, as a star absorbs the night.

VARIANT

Sometimes a word will start it, like
Hands and feet, sun and gloves. The way
Is fraught with danger, you say, and I
Notice the word "fraught" as you are telling
Me about huge secret valleys some distance from
The mired fighting—"but always, lightly wooded
As they are, more deeply involved with the outcome
That will someday paste a black, bleeding label
In the sky, but until then
The echo, flowing freely in corridors, alleys,
And tame, surprised places far from anywhere,
Will be automatically locked out—*vox
Clamans*—do you see? End of tomorrow.
Don't try to start the car or look deeper
Into the eternal wimpling of the sky: luster
On luster, transparency floated onto the topmost layer
Until the whole thing overflows like a silver
Wedding cake or Christmas tree, in a cascade of tears."

WOODEN BUILDINGS

The tests are good. You need a million of them.
You'd die laughing as I write to you
Through leaves and articulations, yes, laughing
Myself silly too. The funniest little thing . . .

That's how it all began. Looking back on it,
I wonder now if it could have been on some day
Findable in an old calendar? But no,
It wasn't out of history, but inside it.
That's the thing. On whatever day we came
To a small house built just above the water,
You had to stoop over to see inside the attic window.
Someone had judged the height to be just right
The way the light came in, and they are
Giving that party, to turn on that dishwasher
And we may be led, then, upward through more
Powerful forms of poetry, past columns
With peeling posters on them, to the country of indifference.
Meanwhile if the swell diapasons, blooms
Unhappily and too soon, the little people are nonetheless real.

PYROGRAPHY

Out here on Cottage Grove it matters. The galloping
Wind balks at its shadow. The carriages
Are drawn forward under a sky of fumed oak.
This is America calling:
The mirroring of state to state,
Of voice to voice on the wires,
The force of colloquial greetings like golden
Pollen sinking on the afternoon breeze.
In service stairs the sweet corruption thrives;
The page of dusk turns like a creaking revolving stage in Warren, Ohio.

If this is the way it is let's leave,
They agree, and soon the slow boxcar journey begins,
Gradually accelerating until the gyrating fans of suburbs
Enfolding the darkness of cities are remembered
Only as a recurring tic. And midway
We meet the disappointed, returning ones, without its
Being able to stop us in the headlong night
Toward the nothing of the coast. At Bolinas
The houses doze and seem to wonder why through the
Pacific haze, and the dreams alternately glow and grow dull.
Why be hanging on here? Like kites, circling,
Slipping on a ramp of air, but always circling?

But the variable cloudiness is pouring it on,
Flooding back to you like the meaning of a joke.
The land wasn't immediately appealing; we built it
Partly over with fake ruins, in the image of ourselves:
An arch that terminates in mid-keystone, a crumbling stone pier
For laundresses, an open-air theater, never completed
And only partially designed. How are we to inhabit
This space from which the fourth wall is invariably missing,
As in a stage-set or dollhouse, except by staying as we are,
In lost profile, facing the stars, with dozens of as yet

Unrealized projects, and a strict sense
Of time running out, of evening presenting
The tactfully folded-over bill? And we fit
Rather too easily into it, become transparent,
Almost ghosts. One day
The birds and animals in the pasture have absorbed
The color, the density of the surroundings,
The leaves are alive, and too heavy with life.

A long period of adjustment followed.
In the cities at the turn of the century they knew about it
But were careful not to let on as the iceman and the milkman
Disappeared down the block and the postman shouted
His daily rounds. The children under the trees knew it
But all the fathers returning home
On streetcars after a satisfying day at the office undid it:
The climate was still floral and all the wallpaper
In a million homes all over the land conspired to hide it.
One day we thought of painted furniture, of how
It just slightly changes everything in the room
And in the yard outside, and how, if we were going
To be able to write the history of our time, starting with today,
It would be necessary to model all these unimportant details
So as to be able to include them; otherwise the narrative
Would have that flat, sandpapered look the sky gets
Out in the middle west toward the end of summer,
The look of wanting to back out before the argument
Has been resolved, and at the same time to save appearances
So that tomorrow will be pure. Therefore, since we have to do our business
In spite of things, why not make it in spite of everything?
That way, maybe the feeble lakes and swamps
Of the back country will get plugged into the circuit
And not just the major events but the whole incredible
Mass of everything happening simultaneously and pairing off,

Channeling itself into history, will unroll
As carefully and as casually as a conversation in the next room,
And the purity of today will invest us like a breeze,
Only be hard, spare, ironical: something one can
Tip one's hat to and still get some use out of.

The parade is turning into our street.
My stars, the burnished uniforms and prismatic
Features of this instant belong here. The land
Is pulling away from the magic, glittering coastal towns
To an aforementioned rendezvous with August and December.
The hunch is it will always be this way,
The look, the way things first scared you
In the night light, and later turned out to be,
Yet still capable, all the same, of a narrow fidelity
To what you and they wanted to become:
No sighs like Russian music, only a vast unravelling
Out toward the junctions and to the darkness beyond
To these bare fields, built at today's expense.

THE GAZING GRAIN

The tires slowly came to a rubbery stop.
Alliterative festoons in the sky noted
That this branchy birthplace of presidents was also
The big frigidaire-cum-cowbarn where mendicant

And margrave alike waited out the results
Of the natural elections. So any openness of song
Was the plainer way. O take me to the banks
Of your Mississippi over there, etc. Like a plant

Rooted in parched earth I am
A stranger myself in the dramatic lighting,
The result of war. That which is given to see
At any moment is the residue, shadowed

In gold or emerging into the clear bluish haze
Of uncertainty. We come back to ourselves
Through the rubbish of cloud and tree-spattered pavement.
These days stand like vapor under the trees.

UNCTUOUS PLATITUDES

There is no reason for the surcharge to bother you.
Living in a city one is nonplussed by some

Of the inhabitants. The weather has grown gray with age.
Poltergeists go about their business, sometimes

Demanding a sweeping revision. The breath of the air
Is invisible. People stay

Next to the edges of fields, hoping that out of nothing
Something will come, and it does, but what? Embers

Of the rain tamp down the shitty darkness that issues
From nowhere. A man in her room, you say.

I like the really wonderful way you express things
So that it might be said, that of all the ways in which to

Emphasize a posture or a particular mental climate
Like this gray-violet one with a thin white irregular line

Descending the two vertical sides, these are those which
Can also unsay an infinite number of pauses

In the ceramic day. Every invitation
To every stranger is met at the station.

THE COUPLE IN THE NEXT ROOM

She liked the blue drapes. They made a star
At the angle. A boy in leather moved in.
Later they found names from the turn of the century
Coming home one evening. The whole of being
Unknown absorbed into the stalk. A free
Bride on the rails warning to notice other
Hers and the great graves that outwore them
Like faces on a building, the lightning rod
Of a name calibrated all their musing differences.

Another day. Deliberations are recessed
In an iron-blue chamber of that afternoon
On which we wore things and looked well at
A slab of business rising behind the stars.

BUSINESS PERSONALS

The disquieting muses again: what are "leftovers"?
Perhaps they have names for it all, who come bearing
Worn signs of privilege whose authority
Speaks out of the accumulation of age and faded colors
To the center of today. Floating heart, why
Wander on senselessly? The tall guardians
Of yesterday are steep as cliff shadows;
Whatever path you take abounds in their sense.
All presently lead downward, to the harbor view.

Therefore do your knees need to be made strong, by running.
We have places for the training and a special on equipment:
Knee-pads, balancing poles and the rest. It works
In the sense of aging: you come out always a little ahead
And not so far as to lose a sense of the crowd
Of disciples. That were tyranny,
Outrage, hubris. Meanwhile this tent is silence
Itself. Its walls are opaque, so as not to see
The road; a pleasant, half-heard melody climbs to its ceiling—
Not peace, but rest the doctor ordered. Tomorrow . . .
And songs climb out of the flames of the near campfires,
Pale, pastel things exquisite in their frailness
With a note or two to indicate it isn't lost,
On them at least. The songs decorate our notion of the world
And mark its limits, like a frieze of soap-bubbles.

What caused us to start caring?
In the beginning was only sedge, a field of water
Wrinkled by the wind. Slowly
The trees increased the novelty of always being alone,
The rest began to be sketched in, and then . . . silence,
Or blankness, for a number of years. Could one return
To the idea of nature summed up in these pastoral images?
Yet the present has done its work of building

A rampart against the past, not a rampart,
A barbed-wire fence. So now we know
What occupations to stick to (scrimshaw, spinning tall tales)
By the way the songs deepen the color of the shadow
Impregnating your hobby as you bend over it,
Squinting. I could make a list
Of each one of my possessions and the direction it
Pointed in, how much each thing cost, how much for wood, string, colored
    ink, etc.

The song makes no mention of directions.
At most it twists the longitude lines overhead
Like twigs to form a crude shelter. (The ship
Hasn't arrived, it was only a dream. It's somewhere near
Cape Horn, despite all the efforts of Boreas to puff out
Those drooping sails.) The idea of great distance
Is permitted, even implicit in the slow dripping
Of a lute. How to get out?
This giant will never let us out unless we blind him.

And that's how, one day, I got home.
Don't be shocked that the old walls
Hang in rags now, that the rainbow has hardened
Into a permanent late afternoon that elicits too-long
Shadows and indiscretions from the bottom
Of the soul. Such simple things,
And we make of them something so complex it defeats us,
Almost. Why can't everything be simple again,
Like the first words of the first song as they occurred
To one who, rapt, wrote them down and later sang them:
"Only danger deflects
The arrow from the center of the persimmon disc,
Its final resting place. And should you be addressing yourself
To danger? When it takes the form of bleachers

Sparsely occupied by an audience which has
Already witnessed the events of which you write,
Tellingly, in your log? Properly acknowledged
It will dissipate like the pale pink and blue handkerchiefs
That vanished centuries ago into the blue dome
That surrounds us, but which are, some maintain, still here."

CRAZY WEATHER

It's this crazy weather we've been having:
Falling forward one minute, lying down the next
Among the loose grasses and soft, white, nameless flowers.
People have been making a garment out of it,
Stitching the white of lilacs together with lightning
At some anonymous crossroads. The sky calls
To the deaf earth. The proverbial disarray
Of morning corrects itself as you stand up.
You are wearing a text. The lines
Droop to your shoelaces and I shall never want or need
Any other literature than this poetry of mud
And ambitious reminiscences of times when it came easily
Through the then woods and ploughed fields and had
A simple unconscious dignity we can never hope to
Approximate now except in narrow ravines nobody
Will inspect where some late sample of the rare,
Uninteresting specimen might still be putting out shoots, for all we know.

ON THE TOWPATH

At the sign "Fred Muffin's Antiques" they turned off the road into a
   narrow lane lined with shabby houses.

If the thirst would subside just for awhile
It would be a little bit, enough.
This has happened.
The insipid chiming of the seconds
Has given way to an arc of silence
So old it had never ceased to exist
On the roofs of buildings, in the sky.

The ground is tentative.
The pygmies and jacaranda that were here yesterday
Are back today, only less so.
It is a barrier of fact
Shielding the sky from the earth.

On the earth a many-colored tower of longing rises.
There are many ads (to help pay for all this).
Something interesting is happening on every landing.
Ladies of the Second Empire gotten up as characters from Perrault:
Red Riding Hood, Cinderella, the Sleeping Beauty,
Are silhouetted against the stained-glass windows.
A white figure runs to the edge of some rampart
In a hurry only to observe the distance,
And having done so, drops back into the mass
Of clock-faces, spires, stalactite machicolations.
It was the walking sideways, visible from far away,
That told what it was to be known
And kept, as a secret is known and kept.

The sun fades like the spreading
Of a peacock's tail, as though twilight
Might be read as a warning to those desperate

For easy solutions. This scalp of night
Doesn't continue or break off the vacuous chatter
That went on, off and on, all day:
That there could be rain, and
That it could be like lines, ruled lines scored
Across the garden of violet cabbages,
That these and other things could stay on
Longer, though not forever of course;
That other commensals might replace them
And leave in their turn. No,

We aren't meaning that any more.
The question has been asked
As though an immense natural bridge had been
Strung across the landscape to any point you wanted.
The ellipse is as aimless as that,
Stretching invisibly into the future so as to reappear
In our present. Its flexing is its account,
Return to the point of no return.

BIRD'S-EYE VIEW
OF THE TOOL AND DIE CO.

For a long time I used to get up early.
20-30 vision, hemorrhoids intact, he checks into the
Enclosure of time familiarizing dreams
For better or worse. The edges rub off,
The slant gets lost. Whatever the villagers
Are celebrating with less conviction is
The less you. Index of own organ-music playing,
Machinations over the architecture (too
Light to make much of a dent) against meditated
Gang-wars, ice cream, loss, palm terrain.

Under and around the quick background,
Surface is improvisation. The force of
Living hopelessly backward into a past of striped
Conversations. As long as none of them ends this side
Of the mirrored desert in terrorist chorales.
The finest car is as the simplest home off the coast
Of all small cliffs too short to be haze. You turn
To speak to someone beside the dock and the lighthouse
Shines like garnets. It has become a stricture.

WET CASEMENTS

When Eduard Raban, coming along the passage,
walked into the open doorway, he saw that it was
raining. It was not raining much.
  KAFKA, *Wedding Preparations in the Country*

The concept is interesting: to see, as though reflected
In streaming windowpanes, the look of others through
Their own eyes. A digest of their correct impressions of
Their self-analytical attitudes overlaid by your
Ghostly transparent face. You in falbalas
Of some distant but not too distant era, the cosmetics,
The shoes perfectly pointed, drifting (how long you
Have been drifting; how long I have too for that matter)
Like a bottle-imp toward a surface which can never be approached,
Never pierced through into the timeless energy of a present
Which would have its own opinions on these matters,
Are an epistemological snapshot of the processes
That first mentioned your name at some crowded cocktail
Party long ago, and someone (not the person addressed)
Overheard it and carried that name around in his wallet
For years as the wallet crumbled and bills slid in
And out of it. I want that information very much today,

Can't have it, and this makes me angry.
I shall use my anger to build a bridge like that
Of Avignon, on which people may dance for the feeling
Of dancing on a bridge. I shall at last see my complete face
Reflected not in the water but in the worn stone floor of my bridge.

I shall keep to myself.
I shall not repeat others' comments about me.

SAYING IT TO KEEP IT FROM HAPPENING

Some departure from the norm
Will occur as time grows more open about it.
The consensus gradually changed; nobody
Lies about it any more. Rust dark pouring
Over the body, changing it without decay—
People with too many things on their minds, but we live
In the interstices, between a vacant stare and the ceiling,
Our lives remind us. Finally this is consciousness
And the other livers of it get off at the same stop.
How careless. Yet in the end each of us
Is seen to have traveled the same distance—it's time
That counts, and how deeply you have invested in it,
Crossing the street of an event, as though coming out of it were
The same as making it happen. You're not sorry,
Of course, especially if this was the way it had to happen,
Yet would like an exacter share, something about time
That only a clock can tell you: how it feels, not what it means.
It is a long field, and we know only the far end of it,
Not the part we presumably had to go through to get there.
If it isn't enough, take the idea
Inherent in the day, armloads of wheat and flowers
Lying around flat on handtrucks, if maybe it means more
In pertaining to you, yet what is is what happens in the end
As though you cared. The event combined with
Beams leading up to it for the look of force adapted to the wiser
Usages of age, but it's both there
And not there, like washing or sawdust in the sunlight,
At the back of the mind, where we live now.

DAFFY DUCK IN HOLLYWOOD

Something strange is creeping across me.
La Celestina has only to warble the first few bars
Of "I Thought about You" or something mellow from
Amadigi di Gaula for everything—a mint-condition can
Of Rumford's Baking Powder, a celluloid earring, Speedy
Gonzales, the latest from Helen Topping Miller's fertile
Escritoire, a sheaf of suggestive pix on greige, deckle-edged
Stock—to come clattering through the rainbow trellis
Where Pistachio Avenue rams the 2300 block of Highland
Fling Terrace. He promised he'd get me out of this one,
That mean old cartoonist, but just look what he's
Done to me now! I scarce dare approach me mug's attenuated
Reflection in yon hubcap, so jaundiced, so *déconfit*
Are its lineaments—fun, no doubt, for some quack phrenologist's
Fern-clogged waiting room, but hardly what you'd call
Companionable. But everything is getting choked to the point of
Silence. Just now a magnetic storm hung in the swatch of sky
Over the Fudds' garage, reducing it—drastically—
To the aura of a plumbago-blue log cabin on
A Gadsden Purchase commemorative cover. Suddenly all is
Loathing. I don't want to go back inside any more. You meet
Enough vague people on this emerald traffic-island—no,
Not people, comings and goings, more: mutterings, splatterings,
The bizarrely but effectively equipped infantries of happy-go-nutty
Vegetal jacqueries, plumed, pointed at the little
White cardboard castle over the mill run. "Up
The lazy river, how happy we could be?"
How will it end? That geranium glow
Over Anaheim's had the riot act read to it by the
Etna-size firecracker that exploded last minute into
A *carte du Tendre* in whose lower right-hand corner
(Hard by the jock-itch sand-trap that skirts
The asparagus patch of algolagnic *nuits blanches*) Amadis
Is cozening the Princesse de Clèves into a midnight micturition spree

On the Tamigi with the Wallets (Walt, Blossom, and little
Skeezix) on a lamé barge "borrowed" from Ollie
Of the Movies' dread mistress of the robes. Wait!
I have an announcement! This wide, tepidly meandering,
Civilized Lethe (one can barely make out the maypoles
And *châlets de nécessité* on its sedgy shore) leads to Tophet, that
Landfill-haunted, not-so-residential resort from which
Some travellers return! This whole moment is the groin
Of a borborygmic giant who even now
Is rolling over on us in his sleep. Farewell bocages,
Tanneries, water-meadows. The allegory comes unsnarled
Too soon; a shower of pecky acajou harpoons is
About all there is to be noted between tornadoes. I have
Only my intermittent life in your thoughts to live
Which is like thinking in another language. Everything
Depends on whether somebody reminds you of me.
That this is a fabulation, and that those "other times"
Are in fact the silences of the soul, picked out in
Diamonds on stygian velvet, matters less than it should.
Prodigies of timing may be arranged to convince them
We live in one dimension, they in ours. While I
Abroad through all the coasts of dark destruction seek
Deliverance for us all, think in that language: its
Grammar, though tortured, offers pavilions
At each new parting of the ways. Pastel
Ambulances scoop up the quick and hie them to hospitals.
"It's all bits and pieces, spangles, patches, really; nothing
Stands alone. What happened to creative evolution?"
Sighed Aglavaine. Then to her Sélysette: "If his
Achievement is only to end up less boring than the others,
What's keeping us here? Why not leave at once?
I have to stay here while they sit in there,
Laugh, drink, have fine time. In my day
One lay under the tough green leaves,

Pretending not to notice how they bled into
The sky's aqua, the wafted-away no-color of regions supposed
Not to concern us. And so we too
Came where the others came: nights of physical endurance,
Or if, by day, our behavior was anarchically
Correct, at least by New Brutalism standards, all then
Grew taciturn by previous agreement. We were spirited
Away *en bateau*, under cover of fudge dark.
It's not the incomplete importunes, but the spookiness
Of the finished product. True, to ask less were folly, yet
If he is the result of himself, how much the better
For him we ought to be! And how little, finally,
We take this into account! Is the puckered garance satin
Of a case that once held a brace of dueling pistols our
Only acknowledging of that color? I like not this,
Methinks, yet this disappointing sequel to ourselves
Has been applauded in London and St. Petersburg. Somewhere
Ravens pray for us."
                              The storm finished brewing. And thus
She questioned all who came in at the great gate, but none
She found who ever heard of Amadis,
Nor of stern Aureng-Zebe, his first love. Some
There were to whom this mattered not a jot: since all
By definition is completeness (so
In utter darkness they reasoned), why not
Accept it as it pleases to reveal itself? As when
Low skyscrapers from lower-hanging clouds reveal
A turret there, an art-deco escarpment here, and last perhaps
The pattern that may carry the sense, but
Stays hidden in the mysteries of pagination.
Not what we see but how we see it matters; all's
Alike, the same, and we greet him who announces
The change as we would greet the change itself.
All life is but a figment; conversely, the tiny

Tome that slips from your hand is not perhaps the
Missing link in this invisible picnic whose leverage
Shrouds our sense of it. Therefore bivouac we
On this great, blond highway, unimpeded by
Veiled scruples, worn conundrums. Morning is
Impermanent. Grab sex things, swing up
Over the horizon like a boy
On a fishing expedition. No one really knows
Or cares whether this is the whole of which parts
Were vouchsafed—once—but to be ambling on's
The tradition more than the safekeeping of it. This mulch for
Play keeps them interested and busy while the big,
Vaguer stuff can decide what it wants—what maps, what
Model cities, how much waste space. Life, our
Life anyway, is between. We don't mind
Or notice any more that the sky *is* green, a parrot
One, but have our earnest where it chances on us,
Disingenuous, intrigued, inviting more,
Always invoking the echo, a summer's day.

HOUSEBOAT DAYS

"The skin is broken. The hotel breakfast china
Poking ahead to the last week in August, not really
Very much at all, found the land where you began . . ."
The hills smouldered up blue that day, again
You walk five feet along the shore, and you duck
As a common heresy sweeps over. We can botanize
About this for centuries, and the little dazey
Blooms again in the cities. The mind
Is so hospitable, taking in everything
Like boarders, and you don't see until
It's all over how little there was to learn
Once the stench of knowledge has dissipated, and the trouvailles
Of every one of the senses fallen back. Really, he
Said, that insincerity of reasoning on behalf of one's
Sincere convictions, true or false in themselves
As the case may be, to which, if we are unwise enough
To argue at all with each other, we must be tempted
At times—do you see where it leads? To pain,
And the triumph over pain, still hidden
In these low-lying hills which rob us
Of all privacy, as though one were always about to meet
One's double through the chain of cigar smoke
And then it . . . happens, like an explosion in the brain,
Only it's a catastrophe on another planet to which
One has been invited, and as surely cannot refuse:
Pain in the cistern, in the gutters, and if we merely
Wait awhile, that denial, as though a universe of pain
Had been created just so as to deny its own existence.
But I don't set much stock in things
Beyond the weather and the certainties of living and dying:
The rest is optional. To praise this, blame that,
Leads one subtly away from the beginning, where
We must stay, in motion. To flash light
Into the house within, its many chambers,

Its memories and associations, upon its inscribed
And pictured walls, argues enough that life is various.
Life is beautiful. He who reads that
As in the window of some distant, speeding train
Knows what he wants, and what will befall.

Pinpricks of rain fall again.
And from across the quite wide median with its
Little white flowers, a reply is broadcast:
"Dissolve parliament. Hold new elections."
It would be deplorable if the rain also washed away
This profile at the window that moves, and moves on,
Knowing that it moves, and knows nothing else. It is the light
At the end of the tunnel as it might be seen
By him looking out somberly at the shower,
The picture of hope a dying man might turn away from,
Realizing that hope is something else, something concrete
You can't have. So, winding past certain pillars
Until you get to evening's malachite one, it becomes a vast dream
Of having that can topple governments, level towns and cities
With the pressure of sleep building up behind it.
The surge creates its own edge
And you must proceed this way: mornings of assent,
Indifferent noons leading to the ripple of the question
Of late afternoon projected into evening.
Arabesques and runnels are the result
Over the public address system, on the seismograph at Berkeley.
A little simple arithmetic tells you that to be with you
In this passage, this movement, is what the instance costs:
A sail out of some afternoon, beyond amazement, astonished,
Apparently not tampered with. As the rain gathers and protects
Its own darkness, the place in the slipcover is noticed
For the first and last time, fading like the spine
Of an adventure novel behind glass, behind the teacups.

THE LAMENT UPON THE WATERS

For the disciple nothing had changed. The mood was still
Gray tolerance, as the road marched along
Singing its little song of despair. Once, a cry
Started up out of the hills. That old, puzzling persuasion

Again. Sex was part of this,
And the shock of day turning into night.
Though we always found something delicate (too delicate
For some tastes, perhaps) to touch, to desire.

And we made much of this sort of materiality
That clogged the weight of starlight, made it seem
Fibrous, yet there was a chance in this
To see the present as it never had existed,

Clear and shapeless, in an atmosphere like cut glass.
At Latour-Maubourg you said this was a good thing, and on the steps
Of Métro Jasmin the couriers nodded to us correctly, and the
Pact was sealed in the sky. But now moments surround us

Like a crowd, some inquisitive faces, some hostile ones,
Some enigmatic or turned away to an anterior form of time
Given once and for all. The jetstream inscribes a final flourish
That melts as it stays. The problem isn't how to proceed

But is one of being: whether this ever was, and whose
It shall be. To be starting out, just one step
Off the sidewalk, and as such pulled back into the glittering
Snowstorm of stinging tentacles of how that would be worked out

If we ever work it out. And the voice came back at him
Across the water, rubbing it the wrong way: "Thou
Canst but undo the wrong thou hast done." The sackbuts
Embellish it, and we are never any closer to the collision

Of the waters, the peace of light drowning light,
Grabbing it, holding it up streaming. It is all one. It lies
All around, its new message, guilt, the admission
Of guilt, your new act. Time buys

The receiver, the onlooker of the earlier system, but cannot
Buy back the rest. It is night that fell
At the edge of your footsteps as the music stopped.
And we heard the bells for the first time. It is your chapter, I said.

AND UT PICTURA POESIS *IS HER NAME*

You can't say it that way any more.
Bothered about beauty you have to
Come out into the open, into a clearing,
And rest. Certainly whatever funny happens to you
Is OK. To demand more than this would be strange
Of you, you who have so many lovers,
People who look up to you and are willing
To do things for you, but you think
It's not right, that if they really knew you . . .
So much for self-analysis. Now,
About what to put in your poem-painting:
Flowers are always nice, particularly delphinium.
Names of boys you once knew and their sleds,
Skyrockets are good—do they still exist?
There are a lot of other things of the same quality
As those I've mentioned. Now one must
Find a few important words, and a lot of low-keyed,
Dull-sounding ones. She approached me
About buying her desk. Suddenly the street was
Bananas and the clangor of Japanese instruments.
Humdrum testaments were scattered around. His head
Locked into mine. We were a seesaw. Something
Ought to be written about how this affects
You when you write poetry:
The extreme austerity of an almost empty mind
Colliding with the lush, Rousseau-like foliage of its desire to communicate
Something between breaths, if only for the sake
Of others and their desire to understand you and desert you
For other centers of communication, so that understanding
May begin, and in doing so be undone.

WHAT IS POETRY

The medieval town, with frieze
Of boy scouts from Nagoya? The snow

That came when we wanted it to snow?
Beautiful images? Trying to avoid

Ideas, as in this poem? But we
Go back to them as to a wife, leaving

The mistress we desire? Now they
Will have to believe it

As we believe it. In school
All the thought got combed out:

What was left was like a field.
Shut your eyes, and you can feel it for miles around.

Now open them on a thin vertical path.
It might give us—what?—some flowers soon?

AND OTHERS, VAGUER PRESENCES

Are built out of the meshing of life and space
At the point where we are wholly revealed
In the lozenge-shaped openings. Because
It is argued that these structures address themselves
To exclusively aesthetic concerns, like windmills
On a vast plain. To which it is answered
That there are no other questions than these,
Half squashed in mud, emerging out of the moment
We all live, learning to like it. No sonnet
On this furthest strip of land, no pebbles,

No plants. To extend one's life
All day on the dirty stone of some plaza,
Unaware among the pretty lunging of the wind,
Light and shade, is like coming out of
A coma that is a white, interesting country,
Prepared to lose the main memory in a meeting
By torchlight under the twisted end of the stairs.

THE WRONG KIND OF INSURANCE

I teach in a high school
And see the nurses in some of the hospitals,
And if all teachers are like that
Maybe I can give you a buzz some day,
Maybe we can get together for lunch or coffee or something.

The white marble statues in the auditorium
Are colder to the touch than the rain that falls
Past the post-office inscription about rain or snow
Or gloom of night. I think
About what these archaic meanings mean,
That unfurl like a rope ladder down through history,
To fall at our feet like crocuses.

All of our lives is a rebus
Of little wooden animals painted shy,
Terrific colors, magnificent and horrible,
Close together. The message is learned
The way light at the edge of a beach in autumn is learned.
The seasons are superimposed.
In New York we have winter in August
As they do in Argentina and Australia.
Spring is leafy and cold, autumn pale and dry.
And changes build up
Forever, like birds released into the light
Of an August sky, falling away forever
To define the handful of things we know for sure,
Followed by musical evenings.

Yes, friends, these clouds pulled along on invisible ropes
Are, as you have guessed, merely stage machinery,
And the funny thing is it knows we know
About it and still wants us to go on believing
In what it so unskillfully imitates, and wants

To be loved not for that but for itself:
The murky atmosphere of a park, tattered
Foliage, wise old treetrunks, rainbow tissue-paper wadded
Clouds down near where the perspective
Intersects the sunset, so we may know
We too are somehow impossible, formed of so many
   different things,
Too many to make sense to anybody.
We straggle on as quotients, hard-to-combine
Ingredients, and what continues
Does so with our participation and consent.

Try milk of tears, but it is not the same.
The dandelions will have to know why, and your comic
Dirge routine will be lost on the unfolding sheaves
Of the wind, a lucky one, though it will carry you
Too far, to some manageable, cold, open
Shore of sorrows you expected to reach,
Then leave behind.
                Thus, friend, this distilled,
Dispersed musk of moving around, the product
Of leaf after transparent leaf, of too many
Comings and goings, visitors at all hours.
                     Each night
Is trifoliate, strange to the touch.

FRIENDS

I like to speak in rhymes,
because I am a rhyme myself.
                    NIJINSKY

I saw a cottage in the sky.
I saw a balloon made of lead.
I cannot restrain my tears, and they fall
On my left hand and on my silken tie,
But I cannot and do not want to hold them back.

One day the neighbors complain about an unpleasant odor
Coming from his room. *I went for a walk*
But met no friends. Another time I go outside
Into the world. It rocks on and on.
It was rocking before I saw it
And is presumably doing so still.

The banker lays his hand on mine.
His face is as clean as a white handkerchief.
We talk nonsense as usual.
I trace little circles on the light that comes in
Through the window on saw-horse legs.
Afterwards I see that we are three.
Someone had entered the room while I was discussing my money
    problems.
I wish God would put a stop to this. I
Turn and see the new moon through glass. I am yanked away
So fast I lose my breath, a not unpleasant feeling.

I feel as though I had been carrying the message for years
On my shoulders like Atlas, never feeling it
Because of never having known anything else. In another way
I am involved with the message. I want to put it down
(In two senses of "put it down") so that you

May understand the agreeable destiny that awaits us.
You sigh. Your sighs will admit of no impatience,
Only a vast crater lake, vast as the sea,
In which the sky, smaller than that, is reflected.

I reach for my hat
And am bound to repeat with tact
The formal greeting I am charged with.
No one makes mistakes. No one runs away
Any more. I bite my lip and
Turn to you. Maybe now you understand.

The feeling is a jewel like a pearl.

THE ICE-CREAM WARS

Although I mean it, and project the meaning
As hard as I can into its brushed-metal surface,
It cannot, in this deteriorating climate, pick up
Where I leave off. It sees the Japanese text
(About two men making love on a foam-rubber bed)
As among the most massive secretions of the human spirit.
Its part is in the shade, beyond the iron spikes of the fence,
Mixing red with blue. As the day wears on
Those who come to seem reasonable are shouted down
(*Why you old goat!* Look who's talkin'. Let's see you
Climb off that tower—the waterworks architecture, both
    stupid and
Grandly humorous at the same time, is a kind of mask for him,
Like a seal's face. Time and the weather
Don't always go hand in hand, as here: sometimes
One is slanted sideways, disappears for awhile.
Then later it's forget-me-not time, and rapturous
Clouds appear above the lawn, and the rose tells
The old old story, the pearl of the orient, occluded
And still apt to rise at times.)
                        A few black smudges
On the outer boulevards, like squashed midges
And the truth becomes a hole, something one has always
    known,
A heaviness in the trees, and no one can say
Where it comes from, or how long it will stay—

A randomness, a darkness of one's own.

BLUE SONATA

Long ago was the then beginning to seem like now
As now is but the setting out on a new but still
Undefined way. *That* now, the one once
Seen from far away, is our destiny
No matter what else may happen to us. It is
The present past of which our features,
Our opinions are made. We are half it and we
Care nothing about the rest of it. We
Can see far enough ahead for the rest of us to be
Implicit in the surroundings that twilight is.
We know that this part of the day comes every day
And we feel that, as it has its rights, so
We have our right to be ourselves in the measure
That we are in it and not some other day, or in
Some other place. The time suits us
Just as it fancies itself, but just so far
As we not give up that inch, breath
Of becoming before becoming may be seen,
Or come to seem all that it seems to mean now.

The things that were coming to be talked about
Have come and gone and are still remembered
As being recent. There is a grain of curiosity
At the base of some new thing, that unrolls
Its question mark like a new wave on the shore.
In coming to give, to give up what we had,
We have, we understand, gained or been gained
By what was passing through, bright with the sheen
Of things recently forgotten and revived.
Each image fits into place, with the calm
Of not having too many, of having just enough.
We live in the sigh of our present.

If that was all there was to have
We could re-imagine the other half, deducing it
From the shape of what is seen, thus
Being inserted into its idea of how we
Ought to proceed. It would be tragic to fit
Into the space created by our not having arrived yet,
To utter the speech that belongs there,
For progress occurs through re-inventing
These words from a dim recollection of them,
In violating that space in such a way as
To leave it intact. Yet we do after all
Belong here, and have moved a considerable
Distance; our passing is a facade.
But our understanding of it is justified.

SYRINGA

Orpheus liked the glad personal quality
Of the things beneath the sky. Of course, Eurydice was a part
Of this. Then one day, everything changed. He rends
Rocks into fissures with lament. Gullies, hummocks
Can't withstand it. The sky shudders from one horizon
To the other, almost ready to give up wholeness.
Then Apollo quietly told him: "Leave it all on earth.
Your lute, what point? Why pick at a dull pavan few care to
Follow, except a few birds of dusty feather,
Not vivid performances of the past." But why not?
All other things must change too.
The seasons are no longer what they once were,
But it is the nature of things to be seen only once,
As they happen along, bumping into other things, getting along
Somehow. That's where Orpheus made his mistake.
Of course Eurydice vanished into the shade;
She would have even if he hadn't turned around.
No use standing there like a gray stone toga as the whole wheel
Of recorded history flashes past, struck dumb, unable to utter an
    intelligent
Comment on the most thought-provoking element in its train.
Only love stays on the brain, and something these people,
These other ones, call life. Singing accurately
So that the notes mount straight up out of the well of
Dim noon and rival the tiny, sparkling yellow flowers
Growing around the brink of the quarry, encapsulates
The different weights of the things.
                                        But it isn't enough
To just go on singing. Orpheus realized this
And didn't mind so much about his reward being in heaven
After the Bacchantes had torn him apart, driven
Half out of their minds by his music, what it was doing to
    them.
Some say it was for his treatment of Eurydice.

But probably the music had more to do with it, and
The way music passes, emblematic
Of life and how you cannot isolate a note of it
And say it is good or bad. You must
Wait till it's over. "The end crowns all,"
Meaning also that the "tableau"
Is wrong. For although memories, of a season, for example,
Melt into a single snapshot, one cannot guard, treasure
That stalled moment. It too is flowing, fleeting;
It is a picture of flowing, scenery, though living, mortal,
Over which an abstract action is laid out in blunt,
Harsh strokes. And to ask more than this
Is to become the tossing reeds of that slow,
Powerful stream, the trailing grasses
Playfully tugged at, but to participate in the action
No more than this. Then in the lowering gentian sky
Electric twitches are faintly apparent first, then burst forth
Into a shower of fixed, cream-colored flares. The horses
Have each seen a share of the truth, though each thinks,
"I'm a maverick. Nothing of this is happening to me,
Though I can understand the language of birds, and
The itinerary of the lights caught in the storm is fully
    apparent to me.
Their jousting ends in music much
As trees move more easily in the wind after a summer storm
And is happening in lacy shadows of shore-trees, now, day
    after day."

But how late to be regretting all this, even
Bearing in mind that regrets are always late, too late!
To which Orpheus, a bluish cloud with white contours,
Replies that these are of course not regrets at all,
Merely a careful, scholarly setting down of
Unquestioned facts, a record of pebbles along the way.

And no matter how all this disappeared,
Or got where it was going, it is no longer
Material for a poem. Its subject
Matters too much, and not enough, standing there helplessly
While the poem streaked by, its tail afire, a bad
Comet screaming hate and disaster, but so turned inward
That the meaning, good or other, can never
Become known. The singer thinks
Constructively, builds up his chant in progressive stages
Like a skyscraper, but at the last minute turns away.
The song is engulfed in an instant in blackness
Which must in turn flood the whole continent
With blackness, for it cannot see. The singer
Must then pass out of sight, not even relieved
Of the evil burthen of the words. Stellification
Is for the few, and comes about much later
When all record of these people and their lives
Has disappeared into libraries, onto microfilm.
A few are still interested in them. "But what about
So-and-so?" is still asked on occasion. But they lie
Frozen and out of touch until an arbitrary chorus
Speaks of a totally different incident with a similar name
In whose tale are hidden syllables
Of what happened so long before that
In some small town, one indifferent summer.

From *FANTASIA ON*
"THE NUT-BROWN MAID"

Unless this is the shelf of whatever happens? The cold sunrise attacks one side of the giant capital letters, bestirs a little the landmass as it sinks, grateful but asleep. And you too are a rebus from another century, your fiction in piles like lace, in that a new way of appreciating has been invented, that tomorrow will be quantitatively and qualitatively different— young love, cheerful, insubstantial things—and that these notions have been paraded before, though never with the flashing density climbing higher with you on the beanstalk until the jewelled mosaic of hills, ploughed fields and rivers agreed to be so studied and fell away forever, a gash of laughter, a sneeze of gold dust into the prism that weeps and remains solid.

Well had she represented the patient's history to his apathetic scrutiny. Always there was something to see, something going on, *for the historical past owed it to itself, our historical present.* There were visiting firemen, rumors of chattels on a spree, old men made up to look like young women in the polygon of night from which light sometimes breaks, to be sucked back, armies of foreigners who could not understand each other, the sickening hush just before the bleachers collapse, the inevitable uninvited and only guest who writes on the wall: I choose not to believe. It became a part of oral history. Things overheard in cafés assumed an importance previously reserved for letters from the front. The past was a dream of doctors and drugs. This wasn't misspent time. Oh, sometimes it'd seem like doing the same thing over and over, until I had passed beyond whatever the sense of it had been. Besides, hadn't it all ended a long time back, on some clear, washed-out afternoon, with a stiff breeze that seemed to shout: go back! For the moated past lives by these dreams of decorum that take into account any wisecracks made at their expense. It is not called living in a past. If history were only minding one's business, but, once under the gray shade of mist drawn across us . . . And who am I to speak this way, into a shoe? I know that evening is busy with lights, cars . . . That the curve will include me if I must stand here. My warm regards are cold, falling back to the vase again like a fountain. Responsible to whom? I have chosen this environment and it is handsome: a festive ruching of bare twigs against the sky, masks under the balconies

that

I sing alway

From
AS
WE
KNOW

From *LITANY*

Some certified nut
Will try to tell you it's poetry,
(It's extraordinary, it makes a great deal of sense)
But watch out or he'll start with some
New notion or other and switch to both
Leaving you wiser and not emptier though
Standing on the edge of a hill.
We have to worry
About systems and devices there is no
Energy here no spleen either
We have to take over the sewer plans—
Otherwise the coursing clear water, planes
Upon planes of it, will have its day
And disappear. Same goes for business:
Holed up in some office skyscraper it's
Often busy to predict the future for business plans
But try doing it from down
In the street and see how far it gets you! You
Really have to sequester yourself to see
How far you have come but I'm
Not going to talk about that.

I'm fairly well pleased
With the way you and I have come around the hill
Ignoring and then anointing its edge even if
We felt it keenly in the backwind.
You were a secretary at first until it
Came time to believe you and then the black man
Replaced your headlights with fuel
You seemed to grow from no place. And now,
Calmed down, like a Corinthian column
You grow and grow, scaling the high plinths
Of the sky.

Others, the tenor, the doctor,
Want us to walk about on it to see how we feel
About it before they attempt anything, yet
In whose house are we? Must we not sit
Quietly, for we would not do this at home?
A splattering of trumpets against the very high
Pockmarked wall and a forgetting of spiny
Palm trees and it is over for us all,
Not just us, and yet on the inside it was
Doomed to happen again, over and over, like a
Wave on a beach, that thinks it's had this
Tremendous idea, coming to crash on the beach
Like that, and it's true, it has, yet
Others have gone before, and still others will
Follow, and far from undermining the spiciness
Of this individual act, this knowledge plants
A seed of eternal endeavor for fear of
Happening just once, and goes on this way,
And yet the originality should not deter
Our vision from the drain
That absorbs, night and day, all our equations,
Makes us brittle, emancipated, not men in a word.
Dying of fright
In the violet night you come to understand how it
Looked to the ancestors and what there was about it
That moved them and are come no closer
To the divine riddle which is aging,
So beautiful in the eternal honey of the sun
And spurs us on to a higher pitch
Of elocution that the company
Will not buy, and so back to our grandstand
Seat with the feeling of having mended
The contrary principles with the catgut
Of abstract sleek ideas that come only once in

The night to be born and are gone forever after
Leaving their trace after the stitches have
Been removed but who is to say they are
Traces of what really went on and not
Today's palimpsest? For what
Is remarkable about our chronic reverie (a watch
That is always too slow or too fast)
Is the lively sense of accomplishment that haloes it
From afar. There is no need
To approach closely, it will be done from here
And work out better, you'll see.

So the giant slabs of material
Came to be, and precious little else, and
No information about them but that was all right
For the present century. Later on
We'd see how it might be in some other
Epoch, but for the time being it was neither
Your nor the population's concern, and may
Have glittered as it declined but for now
It would have to do, as any magic
Is the right kind at the right time.
There is no soothsaying
Yet it happens in rows, windrows
You call them in your far country.

But you are leaving:
Some months ago I got an offer
From Columbia Tape Club, Terre
Haute, Ind., where I could buy one
Tape and get another free. I accept-
Ed the deal, paid for one tape and
Chose a free one. But since I've been
Repeatedly billed for my free tape.

I've written them several times but
Can't straighten it out—would you
Try?

SILHOUETTE

Of how that current ran in, and turned
In the climate of the indecent moment
And became an act,
I may not tell. The road
Ran down there and was afterwards there
So that no further borrowing
Of criticism or the desire to add pleasure
Was ever seen that way again.

In the blank mouths
Of your oppressors, however, much
Was seen to provoke. And the way
Though discontinuous, and intermittent, sometimes
Not heard of for years at a time, did,
Nonetheless, move up, although, to his surprise
It was inside the house,
And always getting narrower.

There is no telling to what lengths,
What mannerisms and fictitious subterranean
Flowerings next to the cement he might have
Been driven. But it all turned out another way.
So cozy, so ornery, tempted always,
Yet not thinking in his 1964 Ford
Of the price of anything, the grapes, and her tantalizing touch
So near that the fish in the aquarium
Hung close to the glass, suspended, yet he never knew her
Except behind the curtain. The catastrophe
Buried in the stair carpet stayed there
And never corrupted anybody.
And one day he grew up, and the horizon
Stammered politely. The sky was like muslin.
And still in the old house no one ever answered the bell.

MANY WAGONS AGO

At first it was as though you had passed,
But then no, I said, he is still here,
Forehead refreshed. A light is kindled. And
Another. But no I said

Nothing in this wide berth of lights like weeds
Stays to listen. Doubled up, fun is inside,
The lair a surface compact with the night.
It needs only one intervention,

A stitch, two, three, and then you see
How it is all false equation planted with
Enchanting blue shrubbery on each terrace
That night produces, and they are backing up.

How easily we could spell if we could follow,
Like thread looped through the eye of a needle,
The grooves of light. It resists. But we stay behind, among them,
The injured, the adored.

AS WE KNOW

All that we see is penetrated by it—
The distant treetops with their steeple (so
Innocent), the stair, the windows' fixed flashing—
Pierced full of holes by the evil that is not evil,
The romance that is not mysterious, the life that is not life,
A present that is elsewhere.

And further in the small capitulations
Of the dance, you rub elbows with it,
Finger it. That day you did it
Was the day you had to stop, because the doing
Involved the whole fabric, there was no other way to appear.
You slid down on your knees
For those precious jewels of spring water
Planted on the moss, before they got soaked up
And you teetered on the edge of this
Calm street with its sidewalks, its traffic,

As though they are coming to get you.
But there was no one in the noon glare,
Only birds like secrets to find out about
And a home to get to, one of these days.

The light that was shadowed then
Was seen to be our lives,
Everything about us that love might wish to examine,
Then put away for a certain length of time, until
The whole is to be reviewed, and we turned
Toward each other, to each other.
The way we had come was all we could see
And it crept up on us, embarrassed
That there is so much to tell now, really now.

OTHERWISE

I'm glad it didn't offend me
Not astral rain nor the unsponsored irresponsible musings

Of the soul where it exists
To be fed and fussed over
Are really what this trial is about.

It is meant to be the beginning
Yet turns into anthems and bell ropes
Swaying from landlocked clouds
Otherwise into memories.

Which can't stand still and the progress
Is permanent like the preordained bulk
Of the First National Bank

Like fish sauce, but agreeable.

FLOWERING DEATH

Ahead, starting from the far north, it wanders.
Its radish-strong gasoline fumes have probably been
Locked into your sinuses while you were away.
You will have to deliver it.
The flowers exist on the edge of breath, loose,
Having been laid there.
One gives pause to the other,
Or there will be a symmetry about their movements
Through which each is also an individual.

It is their collective blankness, however,
That betrays the notion of a thing not to be destroyed.
In this, how many facts we have fallen through
And still the old façade glimmers there,
A mirage, but permanent. We must first trick the idea
Into being, then dismantle it,
Scattering the pieces on the wind,
So that the old joy, modest as cake, as wine and friendship
Will stay with us at the last, backed by the night
Whose ruse gave it our final meaning.

HAUNTED LANDSCAPE

Something brought them here. It was an outcropping of peace
In the blurred afternoon slope on which so many picnickers
Had left no trace. The hikers then always passed through
And greeted you silently. And down in one corner

Where the sweet william grew and a few other cheap plants
The rhythm became strained, extenuated, as it petered out
Among pots and watering cans and a trowel. There were no
People now but everywhere signs of their recent audible passage.

She had preferred to sidle through the cane and he
To hoe the land in the hope that some day they would grow happy
Contemplating the result: so much fruitfulness. A legend.
He came now in the certainty of her braided greeting,

Sunlight and shadow, and a great sense of what had been cast off
Along the way, to arrive in this notch. Why were the insiders
Secretly amused at their putting up handbills at night?
By day hardly anyone came by and saw them.

They were thinking, too, that this was the right way to begin
A farm that would later have to be uprooted to make way
For the new plains and mountains that would follow after
To be extinguished in turn as the ocean takes over

Where the glacier leaves off and in the thundering of surf
And rock, something, some note or other, gets lost,
And we have this to look back on, not much, but a sign
Of the petty ordering of our days as it was created and led us

By the nose through itself, and now it has happened
And we have it to look at, and have to look at it
For the good it now possesses which has shrunk from the
Outline surrounding it to a little heap or handful near the center.

Others call this old age or stupidity, and we, living
In that commodity, know how only it can enchant the dear soul
Building up dreams through the night that are cast down
At the end with a graceful roar, like chimes swaying out over

The phantom village. It is our best chance of passing
Unnoticed into the dream and all that the outside said about it,
Carrying all that back to the source of so much that was precious.
At one of the later performances you asked why they called
    it a "miracle,"

Since nothing ever happened. That, of course, was the
    miracle
But you wanted to know why so much action took on so
    much life
And still managed to remain itself, aloof, smiling and courteous.
Is that the way life is supposed to happen? We'll probably
    never know

Until its cover turns into us: the eglantine for duress
And long relativity, until it becomes a touch of red under the bridge
At fixed night, and the cries of the wind are viewed as happy, salient.
How could that picture come crashing off the wall when no one was in the
    room?

At least the glass isn't broken. I like the way the stars
Are painted in this one, and those which are painted out.
The door is opening. A man you have never seen enters the room.
He tells you that it is time to go, but that you may stay,

If you wish. You reply that it is one and the same to you.
It was only later, after the house had materialized elsewhere,
That you remembered you forgot to ask him what form the change would
    take.

But it is probably better that way. Now time and the land are
  identical,

Linked forever.

MY EROTIC DOUBLE

He says he doesn't feel like working today.
It's just as well. Here in the shade
Behind the house, protected from street noises,
One can go over all kinds of old feeling,
Throw some away, keep others.
                              The wordplay
Between us gets very intense when there are
Fewer feelings around to confuse things.
Another go-round? No, but the last things
You always find to say are charming, and rescue me
Before the night does. We are afloat
On our dreams as on a barge made of ice,
Shot through with questions and fissures of starlight
That keep us awake, thinking about the dreams
As they are happening. Some occurrence. You said it.

I said it but I can hide it. But I choose not to.
Thank you. You are a very pleasant person.
Thank you. You are too.

TRAIN RISING OUT OF
THE SEA

It is written in the Book of Usable Minutes
That all things have their center in their dying,
That each is discrete and diaphanous and
Has pointed its prow away from the sand for the next trillion years.

After that we may be friends,
Recognizing in each other the precedents that make us truly
  social.
Do you hear the wind? It's not dying,
It's singing, weaving a song about the president saluting the
  trust,

The past in each of us, until so much memory becomes an
  institution,
Through sheer weight, the persistence of it, no,
Not the persistence: that makes it seem a deliberate act
Of duration, much too deliberate for this ingenuous being

Like an era that refuses to come to an end or be born again.
We need more night for the sky, more blue for the daylight
That inundates our remarks before we can make them
Taking away a little bit of us each time

To be deposited elsewhere
In the place of our involvement
With the core that brought excessive flowering this year
Of enormous sunsets and big breezes

That left you feeling too simple
Like an island just off the shore, one of many, that no one
Notices, though it has a certain function, though an abstract one
Built to prevent you from being towed to shore.

LATE ECHO

Alone with our madness and favorite flower
We see that there really is nothing left to write about.
Or rather, it is necessary to write about the same old things
In the same way, repeating the same things over and over
For love to continue and be gradually different.

Beehives and ants have to be reexamined eternally
And the color of the day put in
Hundreds of times and varied from summer to winter
For it to get slowed down to the pace of an authentic
Saraband and huddle there, alive and resting.

Only then can the chronic inattention
Of our lives drape itself around us, conciliatory
And with one eye on those long tan plush shadows
That speak so deeply into our unprepared knowledge
Of ourselves, the talking engines of our day.

AND I'D LOVE YOU
TO BE IN IT

Playing alone, I found the wall.
One side was gray, the other an indelible gray.
The two sides were separated by a third,
Or spirit wall, a coarser gray. The wall
Was chipped and tarnished in places,
Polished in places.

I wanted to put it behind me
By walking beside it until it ended.
This was never done. Meanwhile
I stayed near the wall, touching the two ends.

With all of my power of living
I am forced to lie on the floor.
To have reached the cleansing end of the journey,
Appearances put off forever, in my new life
There is still no freedom, but excitement
Turns in our throats like woodsmoke.

In what skyscraper or hut
I'll finish? Today there are tendrils
Coming through the slats, and milky, yellowy grapes,
A mild game to divert the doorperson
And we are swiftly inside, the resurrection finished.

TAPESTRY

It is difficult to separate the tapestry
From the room or loom which takes precedence over it.
For it must always be frontal and yet to one side.

It insists on this picture of "history"
In the making, because there is no way out of the punishment
It proposes: sight blinded by sunlight.
The seeing taken in with what is seen
In an explosion of sudden awareness of its formal splendor.

The eyesight, seen as inner,
Registers over the impact of itself
Receiving phenomena, and in so doing
Draws an outline, or a blueprint,
Of what was just there: dead on the line.

If it has the form of a blanket, that is because
We are eager, all the same, to be wound in it:
This must be the good of not experiencing it.

But in some other life, which the blanket depicts anyway,
The citizens hold sweet commerce with one another
And pinch the fruit unpestered, as they will,
As words go crying after themselves, leaving the dream
Upended in a puddle somewhere
As though "dead" were just another adjective.

A LOVE POEM

And they have to get it right. We just need
A little happiness, and when the clever things
Are taken up (O has the mouth shaped that letter?
What do we have bearing down on it?) as the last thin curve
("Positively the last," they say) before the dark:
(The sky is pure and faint, the pavement still wet) and

The dripping is in the walls, within sleep
Itself. I mean there is no escape
From me, from it. The night is itself sleep
And what goes on in it, the naming of the wind,
Our notes to each other, always repeated, always the same.

THIS CONFIGURATION

This movie deals with the epidemic of the way we live now.
What an inane cardplayer. And the age may support it.
Each time the rumble of the age
Is an anthill in the distance.

As he slides the first rumpled card
Out of his dirty ruffled shirtfront the cartoon
Of the new age has begun its ascent
Around all of us like a gauze spiral staircase in which
Some stars have been imbedded.

It is the modern trumpets
Who decide the mood or tenor of this cross-section:
Of the people who get up in the morning,
Still half-asleep. That they shouldn't have fun.
But something scary will come
To get them anyway. You might as well linger
On verandas, enjoying life, knowing
The end is essentially unpredictable.
It might be soldiers
Marching all day, millions of them
Past this spot, like the lozenge pattern
Of these walls, like, finally, a kind of sleep.

Or it may be that we are ordinary people
With not unreasonable desires which we can satisfy
From time to time without causing cataclysms
That keep getting louder and more forceful instead of dying
    away.

Or it may be that we and the other people
Confused with us on the sidewalk have entered

A moment of seeming to be natural, expected,
And we see ourselves at the moment we see them:
Figures of an afternoon, of a century they extended.

THEIR DAY

Each act of criticism is general
But, in cutting itself off from all the others,
Explicit enough.

We know how the criticism must be done
On a specific day of the week. Too much matters
About this day. Another day, and the criticism is thrown down
Like trash into a dim, dusty courtyard.

It will be built again. That's all the point
There is to it. And it is built,
In sunlight, this time. All look up to it.
It has changed. It is different. It is still
Cut off from all the other acts of criticism.
From this it draws a tragic strength. Its greatness.

They are constructing pleasure simultaneously
In an adjacent chamber
That occupies the same cube of space as the critic's study.
For this to be pleasure, it must also be called criticism.

It is the very expensive kind
That comes sealed in a bottle. It is music of the second night
That winds up as if to say: Well, you've had it,
And in doing so, you have it.

From these boxed perimeters
We issue forth irregularly. Sometimes in fear,
But mostly with no knowledge of knowing, only a general
But selective feeling that the world had to go on being good to us.
As long as we don't know that
We can live at the square corners of the streets.
The winter does what it can for its children.

A TONE POEM

It is no longer night. But there is a sameness
Of intention, all the same, in the ways
We address it, rude
Color of what an amazing world,
As it goes flat, or rubs off, and this
Is a marvel, we think, and are careful not to go past it.

But it is the same thing we are all seeing,
Our world. Go after it,
Go get it boy, says the man holding the stick.
Eat, says the hunger, and we plunge blindly in again,
Into the chamber behind the thought.
We can hear it, even think it, but can't get disentangled
   from our brains.
Here, I am holding the winning ticket. Over here.
But it is all the same color again, as though the climate
Dyed everything the same color. It's more practical,
Yet the landscape, those billboards, age as rapidly as before.

THE OTHER CINDY

A breeze came to the aid of that wilted day
Where we sat about fuming at projects
With the funds running out, and others
Too simple and unheard-of to create pressure that moment,

Though it was one of these, lurking in the off-guard
Secrecy of a mind like a magazine article, that kept
Proposing, slicing, disposing, a truant idea even
In that kingdom of the blind, that finally would have
Reined in the mad hunt, quietly, and kept us there,
Thinking, not especially dozing any more, until
The truth had revealed itself the way a natural-gas
Storage tank becomes very well known sometime after
Dawn has slipped in
And seems to have been visible all along
Like a canoe route across the great lake on whose shore
One is left trapped, grumbling not so much at bad luck as
Because only this one side of experience is ever revealed.
And that meant something.

Sure, there was more to it
And the haunted houses in those valleys wanted to congratulate
You on your immobility. Too often the adventurous acolyte
Drops permanently from sight in this beautiful country.
There is much to be said in favor of the danger of warding off danger
But if you ever want to return

Though it seems improbable on the face of it
You must master the huge retards and have faith in the slow
Blossoming of haystacks, stairways, walls of convolvulus,
Until the moon can do no more. Exhausted,
You get out of bed. Your project is completed
Though the experiment is a mess. Return the kit
In the smashed cardboard box to the bright, bland

Cities that gave rise to you, you know
The one with the big Woolworth's and postcard-blue sky.
The contest ends at midnight tonight
But you can submit again, and again.

THE PLURAL OF
"JACK-IN-THE-BOX"

How quiet the diversion stands
Beside my gate, and me all eager and no grace:
Until tomorrow with sifting hands
Uncode the sea that brought me to this place,
Discover people with changing face
But the way is wide over stubble and sands,
Wider and not too wide, as a dish in space
Is excellent, conforming to demands

Not yet formulated. Let certain trends
Believe us, and that way give chase
With hounds, and with the hare erase
All knowledge of its coming here. The lands
Are fewer now under the plain blue blanket whose
Birthday keeps them outside at the end.

From
SHADOW
TRAIN

THE PURSUIT OF HAPPINESS

It came about that there was no way of passing
Between the twin partitions that presented
A unified façade, that of a suburban shopping mall
In April. One turned, as one does, to other interests

Such as the tides in the Bay of Fundy. Meanwhile there was one
Who all unseen came creeping at this scale of visions
Like the gigantic specter of a cat towering over tiny mice
About to adjourn the town meeting due to the shadow,

An incisive shadow, too perfect in its outrageous
Regularity to be called to stand trial again,
That every blistered tongue welcomed as the first
Drops scattered by the west wind, and yet, knowing

That it would always ever afterwards be this way
Caused the eyes to faint, the ears to ignore warnings.
We knew how to get by on what comes along, but the idea
Warning, waiting there like a forest, not emptied, beckons.

PUNISHING THE MYTH

At first it came easily, with the knowledge of the shadow line
Picking its way through various landscapes before coming
To stand far from you, to bless you incidentally
In sorting out what was best for it, and most suitable,

Like snow having second thoughts and coming back
To be wary about this, to embellish that, as though life were a party
At which work got done. So we wiggled in our separate positions
And stayed in them for a time. After something has passed

You begin to see yourself as you would look to yourself on a stage,
Appearing to someone. But to whom? Ah, that's just it,
To have the manners, and the look that comes from having a secret
Isn't enough. But that "not enough" isn't to be worn like a livery,

To be briefly noticed, yet among whom should it be seen? I haven't
Thought about these things in years; that's my luck.
In time even the rocks will grow. And if you have curled and dandled
Your innocence once too often, what attitude isn't then really yours?

PARADOXES AND OXYMORONS

This poem is concerned with language on a very plain level.
Look at it talking to you. You look out a window
Or pretend to fidget. You have it but you don't have it.
You miss it, it misses you. You miss each other.

The poem is sad because it wants to be yours, and cannot be.
What's a plain level? It is that and other things,
Bringing a system of them into play. Play?
Well, actually, yes, but I consider play to be

A deeper outside thing, a dreamed role-pattern,
As in the division of grace these long August days
Without proof. Open-ended. And before you know it
It gets lost in the steam and chatter of typewriters.

It has been played once more. I think you exist only
To tease me into doing it, on your level, and then you aren't there
Or have adopted a different attitude. And the poem
Has set me softly down beside you. The poem is you.

ANOTHER CHAIN LETTER

He had had it told to him on the sward
Where the fat men bowl, and told so that no one—
He least of all—might be sure in the days to come
Of the *exact* terms. Then, each turned back

To his business, as is customary on such occasions.
Months and months went by. The green squirearchy
Of the dandelions was falling through the hoop again
And no one, it seemed, had had the presence of mind

To initiate proceedings or stop the wheel
From the number it was backing away from as it stopped:
It was performing prettily; the puncture stayed unseen;
The wilderness seemed to like the eclogue about it

You wrote and performed, but really no one now
Saw any good in the cause, or any guilt. It was a conspiracy
Of right-handed notions. Which is how we all
Became partners in the pastoral doffing, the night we now knew.

THE IVORY TOWER

Another season, proposing a name and a distant resolution.
And, like the wind, all attention. Those thirsting ears,
Climbers on what rickety heights, have swept you
All alone into their confession, for it is as alone

Each of us stands and surveys this empty cell of time. Well,
What is there to do? And so a mysterious creeping motion
Quickens its demonic profile, bringing tears, to these eyes at least,
Tears of excitement. When was the last time you *knew* that?

Yet in the textbooks thereof you keep getting mired
In a backward innocence, although that too is something
That must be owned, together with the rest.
There is always some impurity. Help it along! Make room for it!

So that in the annals of this year be nothing but what is sobering:
A porch built on pilings, far out over the sand. Then it doesn't
Matter that the deaths come in the wrong order. All has been so easily
Written about. And you find the right order after all: play, the streets,
    shopping, time flying.

AT THE INN

It was me here. Though. And whether this
Be rebus or me now, the way the grass is planted—
Red stretching far out to the horizon—
Surely prevails now. I shall return in the dark and be seen,

Be led to my own room by well-intentioned hands,
Placed in a box with a lid whose underside is dark
So as to grow, and shall grow
Taller than plumes out on the ocean,

Grazing historically. And shall see
The end of much learning, and other things
Out of control and it ends too soon, before hanging up.
So, laying his cheek against the dresser's wooden one,

He died making up stories, the ones
Not every child wanted to listen to.
And for a while it seemed that the road back
Was a track bombarded by stubble like a snow.

THE ABSENCE OF A NOBLE PRESENCE

If it was treason it was so well handled that it
Became unimaginable. No, it was ambrosia
In the alley under the stars and not this undiagnosable
Turning, a shadow in the plant of all things

That makes us aware of certain moments,
That the end is not far off since it will occur
In the present and this is the present.
No it was something not very subtle then and yet again

You've got to remember we don't see that much.
We see a portion of eaves dripping in the pastel book
And are aware that everything doesn't count equally—
There is dreaminess and infection in the sum

And since this too is of our everydays
It matters only to the one you are next to
This time, giving you a ride to the station.
It foretells itself, not the hiccup you both notice.

QUALM

Warren G. Harding invented the word "normalcy,"
And the lesser-known "bloviate," meaning, one imagines,
To spout, to spew aimless verbiage. He never wanted to be president.
The "Ohio Gang" made him. He died in the Palace

Hotel in San Francisco, coming back from Alaska,
As his wife was reading to him, about him,
From *The Saturday Evening Post*. Poor Warren. He wasn't a bad egg,
Just weak. He loved women and Ohio.

This protected summer of high, white clouds, a new golf star
Flashes like confetti across the intoxicating early part
Of summer, almost to the end of August. The crowd is hysterical:
Fickle as always, they follow him to the edge

Of the inferno. But the fall is, deliciously, only his.
They shall communicate this and that and compute
Fixed names like "doorstep in the wind." The agony is permanent
Rather than eternal. He'd have noticed it. Poor Warren.

SOMETHING SIMILAR

I, the city mouse, have traveled from a long ways away
To be with you with my news. Now you have my passport
With its color photo in it, to be sweet with you
As the times allow. I didn't say that because it's true,

I said it from a dim upstairs porch into the veiled
Shapely masses of this country you are the geography of
So you can put it in your wallet. That's all we can do
For the time being. Elegance has been halted for the duration

And may not be resumed again. The bare hulk tells us
Something, but mostly about what a strain it was to be brought
To such a pass, and then abandoned. So we may never
Again feel fully confident of the stratagem that bore us

And lived on a certain time after that. And it went away
Little by little, as most things do. To profit
By this mainstream is today's chore and adventure. He
Who touches base first at dusk is possessed first, then wins.

OR IN MY THROAT

To the poet as a basement quilt, but perhaps
To some reader a latticework of regrets, through which
You can see the funny street, with the ends of cars and the dust,
The thing we always forget to put in. For him

The two ends were the same except that he was in one
Looking at the other, and all his grief stemmed from that:
There was no way of appreciating anything else, how polite
People were for instance, and the dream, reversed, became

A swift nightmare of starlight on frozen puddles in some
Dread waste. Yet you always hear
How they are coming along. Someone always has a letter
From one of them, asking to be remembered to the boys, and all.

That's why I quit and took up writing poetry instead.
It's clean, it's relaxing, it doesn't squirt juice all over
Something you were certain of a minute ago and now your own face
Is a stranger and no one can tell you it's true. Hey, stupid!

UNTILTED

How tall the buildings were as I began
To live, and how high the rain that battered them!
Why, coming down them, as I often did at night,
Was a dream even before you reached the first gullies

And gave yourself over to thoughts of your own welfare.
It was the tilt of the wine in the cavalier's tilted glass
That documents so unerringly the faces and the mood in the room.
One slip would not be fatal, but then this is not a win or lose

Situation, so involved with living in the past on the ridge
Of the present, hearing its bells, breathing in its steam. . . .
And the shuttle never falters, but to draw an encouraging conclusion
From this would be considerable, too odd. Why not just

Breathe in with the courage of each day, recognizing yourself as one
Who must with difficulty get down from high places? Forget
The tourists—other people must travel too. It hurts now,
Cradled in the bend of your arm, the pure tear, doesn't it?

THE LEASING OF SEPTEMBER

The sleeping map lay green, and we who were never much
To begin with, except for what the attractiveness of youth
Contributed, stood around in the pastures of heaped-up, thickened
White light, convinced that the story was coming to a close,

Otherwise why all these figurines, the Latin freemasonry in the corners?
You stepped into a blue taxi, and as I swear my eyes were in keeping
With the beauty of you as they saw it, so a swallow perpetuated
In dove-gray dusk can be both the end and the exaltation of a new

Beginning, yet forever remain itself, as you
Seem to run alongside me as the car picks up speed. Is it
Your hand then? Will I always then return
To the tier upon tier of cloth layered in the closet

Against what departure? Even a departure from the normal?
So we are not recognized, under the metal. But to him
The love was a solid object, like a partly unpacked trunk,
As it was then, which is different now when remembered.

UNUSUAL PRECAUTIONS

"We, we children, why our lives are circumscribed, circumferential;
Close, too close to the center, we are haunted by perimeters
And our lives seem to go in and out, in and out all the time,
As though yours were diagonal, vertical, shallow, chopped off

At the root like the voice of the famous gadfly: 'Oh! Aho!' it
Sits in the middle of the roadway. That's it. Worry and brown desk
Stain it by infusion. There aren't enough tags at the end,
And the grove is blind, blossoming, but we are too porous to hear it.

It's like watching a movie of a nightmare, the many episodes
That defuse the thrust of what comes to us. The girl who juggled Indian
  clubs
Belongs again to the paper space that backs the black
Curtain, as though there were a reason to have paid for these seats.

Tomorrow you'll be walking in a white park. Our interests
Are too close for us to see. There seems to be no
Necessity for it, yet in walking, we too, around, and all around
We'll come to one, where the street crosses your name, and feet run up it."

WE HESITATE

The days to come are a watershed.
You have to improve your portrait of God
To make it plain. It is on the list,
You and your bodies are on the line.

The new past now unfurls like a great somber hope
Above the treeline, like a giant's hand
Placed tentatively on the hurrying clouds.
The basins come to be full and complex

But it is not enough. Concern and embarrassment
Grow rank. Once they have come home there is no cursing.
Fires disturb the evening. No one can hear the story.
Or sometimes people just forget

Like a child. It took me months
To get that discipline banned, and what is the use,
To ban that? You remain a sane, yet sophisticated, person:
Rooted in twilight, dreaming, a piece of traffic.

FRONTISPIECE

Expecting rain, the profile of a day
Wears its soul like a hat, prow up
Against the deeply incised clouds and regions
Of abrupt skidding from cold to cold, riddles

Of climate it cannot understand.
Sometimes toward the end
A look of longing broke, taut, from those eyes
Meeting yours in final understanding, late,

And often, too, the beginnings went unnoticed
As though the story could advance its pawns
More discreetly thus, overstepping
The confines of ordinary health and reason

To introduce in another way
Its fact into the picture. It registered,
It must be there. And so we turn the page over
To think of starting. This is all there is.

THE VEGETARIANS

In front of you, long tables leading down to the sun,
A great gesture building. You accept it so as to play with it
And translate when its attention is deflated for the one second
Of eternity. Extreme patience and persistence are required,

Yet everybody succeeds at this before being handed
The surprise box lunch of the rest of his life. But what is
Truly startling is that it all happens modestly in the vein of
True living, and then that too is translated into something

Floating up from it, signals that life flashed, weak but essential
For uncorking the tone, and now lost, recently but forever.
In Zurich everything was pure and purposeful, like the red cars
Swung around the lake on wires, against the sky, then back down

Through the weather. Which resembles what you want to do
No more than black tree trunks do, though you thought of it.
Therefore our legends always come around to seeming legendary,
A path decorated with our comings and goings. Or so I've been told.

From
A WAVE

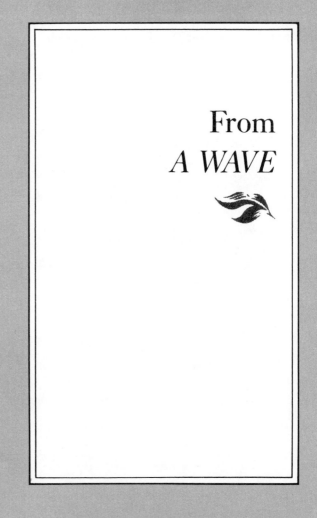

AT NORTH FARM

Somewhere someone is traveling furiously toward you,
At incredible speed, traveling day and night,
Through blizzards and desert heat, across torrents, through narrow passes.
But will he know where to find you,
Recognize you when he sees you,
Give you the thing he has for you?

Hardly anything grows here,
Yet the granaries are bursting with meal,
The sacks of meal piled to the rafters.
The streams run with sweetness, fattening fish;
Birds darken the sky. Is it enough
That the dish of milk is set out at night,
That we think of him sometimes,
Sometimes and always, with mixed feelings?

THE SONGS WE KNOW BEST

Just like a shadow in an empty room
Like a breeze that's pointed from beyond the tomb
Just like a project of which no one tells—
Or didja really think that I was somebody else?

Your clothes and pantlegs lookin' out of shape
Shape of the body over which they drape
Body which has acted in so many scenes
But didja ever think of what that body means?

It is an organ and a vice to some
A necessary evil which we all must shun
To others an abstraction and a piece of meat
But when you're looking out you're in the driver's seat!

No man cares little about fleshly things
They fill him with a silence that spreads in rings
We wish to know more but we are never sated
No wonder some folks think the flesh is overrated!

The things we know now all got learned in school
Try to learn a new thing and you break the rule
Our knowledge isn't much it's just a small amount
But you feel it quick inside you when you're down for the count

You look at me and frown like I was out of place
I guess I never did much for the human race
Just hatched some schemes on paper that looked good at first
Sat around and watched until the bubble burst

And now you're lookin' good all up and down the line
Except for one thing you still have in mind
It's always there though often with a different face
It's the worm inside the jumping bean that makes it race

Too often when you thought you'd be showered with confetti
What they flung at you was a plate of hot spaghetti
You've put your fancy clothes and flashy gems in hock
Yet you pause before your father's door afraid to knock

Once you knew the truth it tried to set you free
And still you stood transfixed just like an apple tree
The truth it came and went and left you in the lurch
And now you think you see it from your lofty perch

The others come and go they're just a dime a dozen
You react to them no more than to a distant cousin
Only a few people can touch your heart
And they too it seems have all gotten a false start

In twilight the city with its hills shines serene
And lets you make of it more than anything could mean
It's the same city by day that seems so crude and calm
You'll have to get to know it not just pump its arm

Even when that bugle sounded loud and clear
You knew it put an end to all your fear
To all that lying and the senseless mistakes
And now you've got it right and you know what it takes

Someday I'll look you up when we're both old and gray
And talk about those times we had so far away
How much it mattered then and how it matters still
Only things look so different when you've got a will

It's true that out of this misunderstanding could end
And men would greet each other like they'd found a friend
With lots of friends around there's no one to entice
And don't you think seduction isn't very nice?

It carries in this room against the painted wall
And hangs in folds of curtains when it's not there at all
It's woven in the flowers of the patterned spread
And lies and knows not what it thinks upon the bed

I wish to come to know you get to know you all
Let your belief in me and me in you stand tall
Just like a project of which no one tells—
Or do ya still think that I'm somebody else?

LANDSCAPE
(After Baudelaire)

I want a bedroom near the sky, an astrologer's cave
Where I can fashion eclogues that are chaste and grave.
Dreaming, I'll hear the wind in the steeples close by
Sweep the solemn hymns away. I'll spy
On factories from my attic window, resting my chin
In both hands, drinking in the songs, the din.
I'll see chimneys and steeples, those masts of the city,
And the huge sky that makes us dream of eternity.

How sweet to watch the birth of the star in the still-blue
Sky, through mist; the lamp burning anew
At the window; rivers of coal climbing the firmament
And the moon pouring out its pale enchantment.
I'll see the spring, the summer and the fall
And when winter casts its monotonous pall
Of snow, I'll draw the blinds and curtains tight
And build my magic palaces in the night;
Then dream of gardens, of bluish horizons,
Of jets of water weeping in alabaster basins,
Of kisses, of birds singing at dawn and at nightfall,
Of all that's most childish in our pastoral.
When the storm rattles my windowpane
I'll stay hunched at my desk, it will roar in vain
For I'll have plunged deep inside the thrill
Of conjuring spring with the force of my will,
Coaxing the sun from my heart, and building here
Out of my fiery thoughts, a tepid atmosphere.

JUST WALKING AROUND

What name do I have for you?
Certainly there is no name for you
In the sense that the stars have names
That somehow fit them. Just walking around,

An object of curiosity to some,
But you are too preoccupied
By the secret smudge in the back of your soul
To say much, and wander around,

Smiling to yourself and others.
It gets to be kind of lonely
But at the same time off-putting,
Counterproductive, as you realize once again

That the longest way is the most efficient way,
The one that looped among islands, and
You always seemed to be traveling in a circle.
And now that the end is near

The segments of the trip swing open like an orange.
There is light in there, and mystery and food.
Come see it. Come not for me but it.
But if I am still there, grant that we may see each other.

THE ONGOING STORY

I could say it's the happiest period of my life.
It hasn't got much competition! Yesterday
It seemed a flatness, hotness. As though it barely stood out
From the rocks of all the years before. Today it sheds
That old name, without assuming any new one. I think it's still there.

It was as though I'd been left with the empty street
A few seconds after the bus pulled out. A dollop of afternoon wind.
Others tell you to take your attention off it
For awhile, refocus the picture. Plan to entertain,
To get out. (Do people really talk that way?)

We could pretend that all that isn't there never existed anyway.
The great ideas? What good are they if they're misplaced,
In the wrong order, if you can't remember one
At the moment you're so to speak mounting the guillotine
Like Sydney Carton, and can't think of anything to say?
Or is this precisely material covered in a course
Called Background of the Great Ideas, and therefore it isn't necessary
To say anything or even know anything? The breath of the moment
Is breathed, we fall and still feel better. The phone rings,

It's a wrong number, and your heart is lighter,
Not having to be faced with the same boring choices again
Which doesn't undermine a feeling for people in general and
Especially in particular: you,
In your deliberate distinctness, whom I love and gladly
Agree to walk blindly into the night with,
Your realness is real to me though I would never take any of it
Just to see how it grows. A knowledge that people live close by is,
I think, enough. And even if only first names are ever exchanged
The people who own them seem rock-true and marvelously self-sufficient.

THANK YOU FOR NOT COOPERATING

Down in the street there are ice-cream parlors to go to
And the pavement is a nice, bluish slate-gray. People laugh a lot.
Here you can see the stars. Two lovers are singing
Separately, from the same rooftop: *"Leave your change behind,*
Leave your clothes, and go. It is time now.
It was time before too, but now it is really time.
You will never have enjoyed storms so much
As on these hot sticky evenings that are more like August
Than September. Stay. A fake wind wills you to go
And out there on the stormy river witness buses bound for Connecticut,
And tree-business, and all that we think about when we stop thinking.
The weather is perfect, the season unclear. Weep for your going
But also expect to meet me in the near future, when I shall disclose
New further adventures, and that you shall continue to think of me."

The wind dropped, and the lovers
Sang no more, communicating each to each in the tedium
Of self-expression, and the shore curled up and became liquid
And so the celebrated lament began. And how shall we, people
All unused to each other and to our own business, explain
It to the shore if it is given to us
To circulate there "in the near future" the why of our coming
And why we were never here before? The counterproposals
Of the guest-stranger impede our construing of ourselves as
Person-objects, the ones we knew would get here
Somehow, but we can remember as easily as the day we were born
The maggots we passed on the way and how the day bled
And the night too on hearing us, though we spoke only our childish
Ideas and never tried to impress anybody even when somewhat older.

MORE PLEASANT ADVENTURES

The first year was like icing.
Then the cake started to show through.
Which was fine, too, except you forget the direction you're taking.
Suddenly you are interested in some new thing
And can't tell how you got here. Then there is confusion
Even out of happiness, like a smoke—
The words get heavy, some topple over, you break others.
And outlines disappear once again.

Heck, it's anybody's story,
A sentimental journey—"gonna take a sentimental journey,"
And we do, but you wake up under the table of a dream:
You are that dream, and it is the seventh layer of you.
We haven't moved an inch, and everything has changed.
We are somewhere near a tennis court at night.
We get lost in life, but life knows where we are.
We can always be found with our associates.
Haven't you always wanted to curl up like a dog and go to sleep like a dog?

In the rash of partings and dyings (the new twist),
There's also room for breaking out of living.
Whatever happens will be quite ingenious.
No acre but will resume being disputed now,
And paintings are one thing we never seem to run out of.

PURISTS WILL OBJECT

We have the looks you want:
The gonzo (musculature seemingly wired to the stars);
Colors like lead, khaki and pomegranate; things you
Put in your hair, with the whole panoply of the past:
Landscape embroidery, complete sets of this and that.
It's bankruptcy, the human haul,
The shining, bulging nets lifted out of the sea, and always a few refugees
Dropping back into the no-longer-mirthful kingdom
On the day someone sells an old house
And someone else begins to add on to his: all
In the interests of this pornographic masterpiece,
Variegated, polluted skyscraper to which all gazes are drawn,
Pleasure we cannot and will not escape.

It seems we were going home.
The smell of blossoming privet blanketed the narrow avenue.
The traffic lights were green and aqueous.
So this is the subterranean life.
If it can't be conjugated onto us, what good is it?
What need for purists when the demotic is built to last,
To outlast us, and no dialect hears us?

37 HAIKU

Old-fashioned shadows hanging down, that difficulty in love too soon

Some star or other went out, and you, thank you for your book and year

Something happened in the garage and I owe it for the blood traffic

Too low for nettles but it is exactly the way people think and feel

And I think there's going to be even more but waist-high

Night occurs dimmer each time with the pieces of light smaller and squarer

You have original artworks hanging on the walls oh I said edit

You nearly undermined the brush I now place against the ball field arguing

That love was a round place and will still be there two years from now

And it is a dream sailing in a dark unprotected cove

Pirates imitate the ways of ordinary people myself for instance

Planted over and over that land has a bitter aftertaste

A blue anchor grains of grit in a tall sky sewing

He is a monster like everyone else but what do you do if you're a monster

Like him feeling him come from far away and then go down to his car

The wedding was enchanted everyone was glad to be in it

What trees, tools, why ponder socks on the premises

Come to the edge of the barn the property really begins there

In a smaller tower shuttered and put away there

You lay aside your hair like a book that is too important to read now

Why did witches pursue the beast from the eight sides of the country

A pencil on glass—shattered! The water runs down the drain

In winter sometimes you see those things and also in summer

A child must go down it must stand and last

Too late the last express passes through the dust of gardens

A vest—there is so much to tell about even in the side rooms

Hesitantly, it built up and passed quickly without unlocking

There are some places kept from the others and are separate, they never exist

I lost my ridiculous accent without acquiring another

In Buffalo, Buffalo she was praying, the nights stick together like pages in an old book

The dreams descend like cranes on gilded, forgetful wings

What is the past, what is it all for? A mental sandwich?

Did you say, hearing the schooner overhead, we turned back to the weir?

In rags and crystals, sometimes with a shred of sense, an odd dignity

The boy must have known the particles fell through the house after him

All in all we were taking our time, the sea returned—no more pirates

I inch and only sometimes as far as the twisted pole gone in spare colors

THE LONEDALE OPERATOR

The first movie I ever saw was the Walt Disney cartoon *The Three Little Pigs*. My grandmother took me to it. It was back in the days when you went "downtown." There was a second feature, with live actors, called *Bring 'Em Back Alive*, a documentary about the explorer Frank Buck. In this film you saw a python swallow a live pig. This wasn't scary. In fact, it seemed quite normal, the sort of thing you *would* see in a movie—"reality."

A little later we went downtown again to see a movie of *Alice in Wonderland*, also with live actors. This wasn't very surprising either. I think I knew something about the story; maybe it had been read to me. That wasn't why it wasn't surprising, though. The reason was that these famous movie actors, like W. C. Fields and Gary Cooper, were playing different roles, and even though I didn't know who they were, they were obviously important for doing other kinds of acting, and so it didn't seem strange that they should be acting in a special way like this, pretending to be characters that people already knew about from a book. In other words, I imagined specialties for them just from having seen this one example. And I was right, too, though not about the film, which I liked. Years later I saw it when I was grown up and thought it was awful. How could I have been wrong the first time? I knew it wasn't inexperience, because somehow I was experienced the first time I saw a movie. It was as though my taste had changed, though I had not, and I still can't help feeling that I was right the first time, when I was still relatively unencumbered by my experience.

I forget what were the next movies I saw and will skip ahead to one I saw when I was grown up, *The Lonedale Operator*, a silent short by D. W. Griffith, made in 1911 and starring Blanche Sweet. Although I was in my twenties when I saw it at the Museum of Modern Art, it seems as remote from me in time as my first viewing of *Alice in Wonderland*. I can remember almost none of it, and the little I can remember may have been in another Griffith short, *The Lonely Villa*, which may have been on the same program. It seems that Blanche Sweet was a heroic telegraph operator who managed to get through to the police and foil some gangsters who were trying to rob a railroad depot, though I also see this living room—small, though it was supposed to be in a large house—with Mary Pickford running around, and this may have been a scene in *The Lonely Villa*. At that moment the memories stop, and terror, or tedium, sets in. It's hard to tell which is which in this memory, because the boredom of living in a lonely place or having a lonely job, and even of being so far in the past and having to wear those funny uncomfortable clothes and hairstyles is terrifying, more so than the intentional scariness of the plot, the criminals, whoever they were.

Imagine that innocence (Lilian Harvey) encounters romance (Willy Fritsch) in the home of experience (Albert Basserman). From there it is only a step to terror, under the dripping boughs outside. Anything can change as fast as it wants to, and in doing so may pass through a more or less terrible phase, but the true terror is in the swiftness of changing, forward or backward, slipping always just beyond our control. The actors are like people on drugs, though they aren't doing anything unusual—as a matter of fact, they are performing brilliantly.

DARLENE'S HOSPITAL

The hospital: it wasn't her idea
That the colors should slide muddy from the brush
And spew their random evocations everywhere,
Provided that things should pick up next season.
It was a way of living, to her way of thinking.
She took a job, it wasn't odd.
But then, backing through the way many minds had been made up,
It came again, the color, always a color
Climbing the apple of the sky, often
A secret lavender place you weren't supposed to look into.
And then a sneeze would come along
Or soon we'd be too far out from shore, on a milky afternoon
Somewhere in late August with the paint flaking off,
The lines of traffic flowing like mucus.
And they won't understand its importance, it's too bad,
Not even when it's too late.

Now we're often happy. The dark car
Moves heftily away along low bluffs,
And if we don't have our feelings, what
Good are we, but whose business is it?
Beware the happy man: once she perched light
In the reading space of my room, a present joy
For all time to come, whatever happens;
And still we rotate, gathering speed until
Nothing is there but more speed in the light ahead.
Such moments as we prized in life:
The promise of a new day, living with lots of people
All headed in more or less the same direction, the sound of this
In the embracing stillness, but not the brutality,
And lists of examples of lots of things, and shit—
What more could we conceivably be satisfied with, it is
Joy, and undaunted

She leaves the earth at that point,
Intersecting all our daydreams of breakfast and lunch.
The Lady of Shalott's in hot water again.

This and the dreams of any of the young
Were not her care. The river flowed
Hard by the hospital from whose gilded
Balconies and turrets fair spirits waved,
Lonely, like us. Here be no pursuers,
Only imagined animals and cries
In the wilderness, which made it "the wilderness,"
And suddenly the lonesomeness becomes a pleasant city
Fanning out around a lake; you get to meet
Precisely the person who would have been here now,
A dream no longer, and are polished and directed
By his deliberate grasp, back
To the reality that was always there despairing
Of your return as months and years went by,
Now silent again forever, the perfect space,
Attuned to your wristwatch
As though time would never go away again.

His dirty mind
Produced it all, an oratorio based on love letters
About our sexual habits in the early 1950s.
It wasn't that these stories weren't true,
Only that a different kind of work
Of the imagination had grown up around them, taller
Than redwoods, and not
Wanting to embarrass them, effaced itself
To the extent that a colossus could, and so you looked
And saw nothing, but suddenly felt better
Without wondering why. And the serial continues:

Pain, expiation, delight, more pain,
A frieze that lengthens continually, in the lucky way
Friezes do, and no plot is produced,
Nothing you could hang an identifying question on.
It's an imitation of pleasure; it may not work
But at least we'll know then that we'll have done
What we could, and chalk it up to virtue
Or just plain laziness. And if she glides
Backwards through us, a finger hooked
Out of death, we shall not know where the mystery began:
Inaccurate dreamers of our state,
Sodden from sitting in the rain too long.

WHATEVER IT IS,
WHEREVER YOU ARE

The cross-hatching technique which allowed our ancestors to exchange certain genetic traits for others, in order to provide their offspring with a way of life at once more variegated and more secure than their own, has just about run out of steam and has left us wondering, once more, what there is about this plush solitude that makes us think we will ever get out, or even want to. The ebony hands of the clock always seem to mark the same hour. That is why it always seems the same, though it is of course changing constantly, subtly, as though fed by an underground stream. If only we could go out in back, as when we were kids, and smoke and fool around and just stay out of the way, for a little while. But that's just it— don't you see? We are "out in back." No one has ever used the front door. We have always lived in this place without a name, without shame, a place for grownups to talk and laugh, having a good time. When we were children it seemed that adulthood would be like climbing a tree, that there would be a view from there, breathtaking because slightly more elusive. But now we can see only down, first down through the branches and further down the surprisingly steep grass patch that slopes away from the base of the tree. It certainly is a different view, but not the one we expected.

What did *they* want us to do? Stand around this way, monitoring every breath, checking each impulse for the return address, wondering constantly about evil until necessarily we fall into a state of torpor that is probably the worst sin of all? To what purpose did they cross-hatch so effectively, so that the luminous surface that was underneath is transformed into another, also luminous but so shifting and so alive with suggestiveness that it is like quicksand, to take a step there would be to fall through the fragile net of uncertainties into the bog of certainty, otherwise known as the Slough of Despond?

Probably they meant for us to enjoy the things they enjoyed, like late summer evenings, and hoped that we'd find others and thank them for providing us with the wherewithal to find and enjoy them. Singing the way they did, in the old time, we can sometimes see through the tissues and tracings the genetic process has laid down between us and them. The tendrils can suggest a hand, or a specific color—the yellow of the tulip, for instance—will flash for a moment in such a way that after it has been withdrawn we can be sure that there was no imagining, no auto-suggestion here, but at the same time it becomes as useless as all subtracted memories. It has brought certainty without heat or light. Yet still in the old time, in the faraway summer evenings, they must have had a word for this, or known that we would someday need one, and wished to help. Then it is that a kind of purring occurs, like the wind sneaking around the baseboards of a room: not the infamous "still, small voice" but an ancillary speech that is parallel to the slithering of our own doubt-fleshed imaginings, a visible soundtrack of the way we sound as we move from encouragement to despair to exasperation and back again, with a gesture sometimes that is like an aborted movement outward toward some cape or promontory from which the view would extend in two directions—backward and forward—but that is only a polite hope in the same vein as all the others, crumpled and put away, and almost not to be distinguished from any of them, except that *it knows we know*, and in the context of not knowing is a fluidity that flashes like silver, that seems to say a film has been exposed and an image will, most certainly will, not like the last time, come to consider itself within the frame.

It must be an old photograph of you, out in the yard, looking almost afraid in the crisp, raking light that afternoons in the city held in those days, unappeased, not accepting anything from anybody. So what else is new? I'll tell you what is: you are accepting this now from the invisible, unknown sender, and the light that was intended, you thought, only to rake or glance is now directed full in your face, as it in fact always was, but you were squinting so hard, fearful of accepting it, that you didn't know this. Whether it warms or burns is another matter, which we will not go into here. The point is that you are accepting it and holding on to it, like love from someone you always thought you couldn't stand, and whom you now recognize as a brother, an equal. Someone whose face is the same as yours in the photograph but who is someone else, all of whose thoughts and feelings are directed at you, falling like a gentle slab of light that will ultimately loosen and dissolve the crusted suspicion, the timely self-hatred,

the efficient cold directness, the horrible good manners, the sensible re-
solves and the senseless nights spent waiting in utter abandon, that have
grown up to be you in the tree with no view; and place you firmly in the
good-natured circle of your ancestors' games and entertainments.

A WAVE

To pass through pain and not know it,
A car door slamming in the night.
To emerge on an invisible terrain.

So the luck of speaking out
A little too late came to be worshipped in various guises:
A mute actor, a future saint intoxicated with the idea of martyrdom;
And our landscape came to be as it is today:
Partially out of focus, some of it too near, the middle distance
A haven of serenity and unreachable, with all kinds of nice
People and plants waking and stretching, calling
Attention to themselves with every artifice of which the human
Genre is capable. And they called it our home.

No one came to take advantage of these early
Reverses, no doorbell rang;
Yet each day of the week, once it had arrived, seemed the threshold
Of love and desperation again. At night it sang
In the black trees: *My mindless, oh my mindless, oh.*
And it could be that it was Tuesday, with dark, restless clouds
And puffs of white smoke against them, and below, the wet streets
That seem so permanent, and all of a sudden the scene changes:
It's another idea, a new conception, something submitted
A long time ago, that only now seems about to work
To destroy at last the ancient network
Of letters, diaries, ads for civilization.
It passes through you, emerges on the other side
And is now a distant city, with all
The possibilities shrouded in a narrative moratorium.
The chroniqueurs who bad-mouthed it, the honest
Citizens whose going down into the day it was,
Are part of it, though none
Stand with you as you mope and thrash your way through time,

Imagining it as it is, a kind of tragic euphoria
In which your spirit sprouted. And which is justified in you.

In the haunted house no quarter is given: in that respect
It's very much business as usual. The reductive principle
Is no longer there, or isn't enforced as much as before.
There will be no getting away from the prospector's
Hunch; past experience matters again; the tale will stretch on
For miles before it is done. There would be more concerts
From now on, and the ground on which a man and his wife could
Look at each other and laugh, remembering how love is to them,
Shrank and promoted a surreal intimacy, like jazz music
Moving over furniture, to say how pleased it was
Or something. In the end only a handshake
Remains, something like a kiss, but fainter. Were we
Making sense? Well, that thirst will account for some
But not all of the marvelous graffiti; meanwhile
The oxygen of the days sketches the rest,
The balance. Our story is no longer alone.
There is a rumbling there
And now it ends, and in a luxurious hermitage
The straws of self-defeat are drawn. The short one wins.

One idea is enough to organize a life and project it
Into unusual but viable forms, but many ideas merely
Lead one thither into a morass of their own good intentions.
Think how many the average person has during the course of a day, or night,
So that they become a luminous backdrop to ever-repeated
Gestures, having no life of their own, but only echoing
The suspicions of their possessor. It's fun to scratch around
And maybe come up with something. But for the tender blur
Of the setting to mean something, words must be ejected bodily,
A certain crispness be avoided in favor of a density
Of strutted opinion doomed to wilt in oblivion: not too linear

Nor yet too puffed and remote. Then the advantage of
Sinking in oneself, crashing through the skylight of one's own
Received opinions redirects the maze, setting up significant
Erections of its own at chosen corners, like gibbets,
And through this the mesmerizing plan of the landscape becomes,
At last, apparent. It is no more a landscape than a golf course is,
Though sensibly a few natural bonuses have been left in. And as it
Focuses itself, it is the backward part of a life that is
Partially coming into view. It's there, like a limb. And the issue
Of making sense becomes such a far-off one. Isn't this "sense"—
This little of my life that I can see—that answers me
Like a dog, and wags its tail, though excitement and fidelity are
About all that ever gets expressed? What did I ever do
To want to wander over into something else, an explanation
Of how I behaved, for instance, when knowing can have this
Sublime rind of excitement, like the shore of a lake in the desert
Blazing with the sunset? So that if it pleases all my constructions
To collapse, I shall at least have had that satisfaction, and known
That it need not be permanent in order to stay alive,
Beaming, confounding with the spell of its good manners.

As with rocks at low tide, a mixed surface is revealed,
More detritus. Still, it is better this way
Than to have to live through a sequence of events acknowledged
In advance in order to get to a primitive statement. And the mind
Is the beach on which the rocks pop up, just a neutral
Support for them in their indignity. They explain
The trials of our age, cleansing it of toxic
Side-effects as it passes through their system.
Reality. Explained. And for seconds
We live in the same body, are a sibling again.

I think all games and disciplines are contained here,
Painting, as they go, dots and asterisks that

We force into meanings that don't concern us
And so leave us behind. But there are no fractions, the world is an integer
Like us, and like us it can neither stand wholly apart nor disappear.
When one is young it seems like a very strange and safe place,
But now that I have changed it feels merely odd, cold
And full of interest. The sofa that was once a seat
Puzzles no longer, while the sweet conversation that occurs
At regular intervals throughout the years is like a collie
One never outgrows. And it happens to you
In this room, it is here, and we can never
Eat of the experience. It drags us down. Much later on
You thought you perceived a purpose in the game at the moment
Another player broke one of the rules; it seemed
A module for the wind, something in which you lose yourself
And are not lost, and then it pleases you to play another day
When outside conditions have changed and only the game
Is fast, perplexed and true, as it comes to have seemed.

Yet one does know why. The covenant we entered
Bears down on us, some are ensnared, and the right way,
It turns out, is the one that goes straight through the house
And out the back. By so many systems
As we are involved in, by just so many
Are we set free on an ocean of language that comes to be
Part of us, as though we would ever get away.
The sky is bright and very wide, and the waves talk to us,
Preparing dreams we'll have to live with and use. The day will come
When we'll have to. But for now
They're useless, more trees in a landscape of trees.

I hadn't expected a glance to be that direct, coming from a sculpture
Of moments, thoughts added on. And I had kept it
Only as a reminder, not out of love. In time I moved on
To become its other side, and then, gentle, anxious, I became as a parent

To those scenes lifted from "real life." There was the quiet time
In the supermarket, and the pieces
Of other people's lives as they sashayed or tramped past
My own section of a corridor, not pausing
In many cases to wonder where they were—maybe they even knew.
True, those things or moments of which one
Finds oneself an enthusiast, a promoter, are few,
But they last well,
Yielding up their appearances for form
Much later than the others. Forgetting about "love"
For a moment puts one miles ahead, on the steppe or desert
Whose precise distance as it feels I
Want to emphasize and estimate. Because
We will all have to walk back this way
A second time, and not to know it then, not
To number each straggling piece of sagebrush
Is to sleep before evening, and well into the night
That always coaxes us out, smooths out our troubles and puts us back to
    bed again.

All those days had a dumb clarity that was about getting out
Into a remembered environment. The headlines and economy
Would refresh for a moment as you look back over the heap
Of rusted box-springs with water under them, and then,
Like sliding up to a door or a peephole a tremendous advantage
Would burst like a bubble. Toys as solemn and knotted as books
Assert themselves first, leading down through a delicate landscape
Of reminders to be better next time to a damp place on my hip,
And this would spell out a warm business letter urging us
All to return to our senses, to the matter of the day
That was ending now. And no special sense of decline ensued
But perhaps a few moments of music of such tact and weariness
That one awakens with a new sense of purpose: more things to be done
And the just-sufficient tools to begin doing them

While awaiting further orders that must materialize soon
Whether in the sand-pit with frightened chickens running around
Or on a large table in a house deep in the country with messages
Pinned to the walls and a sense of plainness quite unlike
Any other waiting. I am prepared to deal with this
While putting together notes related to the question of love
For the many, for two people at once, and for myself
In a time of need unlike those that have arisen so far.
And some day perhaps the discussion that has to come
In order for us to start feeling any of it before we even
Start to think about it will arrive in a new weather
Nobody can imagine but which will happen just as the ages
Have happened without causing total consternation,
Will take place in a night, long before sleep and the love
That comes then, breathing mystery back into all the sterile
Living that had to lead up to it. Moments as clear as water
Splashing on a rock in the sun, though in darkness, and then
Sleep has to affirm it and the body is fresh again,
For the trials and dangerous situations that any love,
However well-meaning, has to use as terms in the argument
That is the reflexive play of our living and being lost
And then changed again, a harmless fantasy that must grow
Progressively serious, and soon state its case succinctly
And dangerously, and we sit down to the table again
Noting the grain of the wood this time and how it pushes through
The pad we are writing on and becomes part of what is written.
Not until it starts to stink does the inevitable happen.

Moving on we approached the top
Of the thing, only it was dark and no one could see,
Only somebody said it was a miracle we had gotten past the
Previous phase, now faced with each other's conflicting
Wishes and the hope for a certain peace, so this would be
Our box and we would stay in it for as long

As we found it comfortable, for the broken desires
Inside were as nothing to the steeply shelving terrain outside,
And morning would arrange everything. So my first impulse
Came, stayed awhile, and left, leaving behind
Nothing of itself, no whisper. The days now move
From left to right and back across this stage and no one
Notices anything unusual. Meanwhile I have turned back
Into that dream of rubble that was the city of our starting out.
No one advises me; the great tenuous clouds of the desert
Sky visit it and they barely touch, so pleasing in the
Immense solitude are the tracks of those who wander and continue
On their route, certain that day will end soon and that night will then fall.

But behind what looks like heaps of slag the peril
Consists in explaining everything too evenly. Those
Suffering from the blahs are unlikely to notice that the topic
Of today's lecture doesn't exist yet, and in their trauma
Will become one with the vast praying audience as it sways and bends
To the rhythm of an almost inaudible piccolo. And when
It is flushed out, the object of all this meditation will not
Infrequently turn out to be a mere footnote to the great chain
That manages only with difficulty to connect earth and sky together.
Are comments like ours really needed? Of course, heaven is nice
About it, not saying anything, but we, when we come away
As children leaving school at four in the afternoon, can we
Hold our heads up and face the night's homework? No, the
Divine tolerance we seem to feel is actually in short supply,
And those moving forward toward us from the other end of the bridge
Are defending, not welcoming us to, the place of power,
A hill ringed with low, ridgelike fortifications. But when
Somebody better prepared crosses over, he or she will get the same
Cold reception. And so because it is impossible to believe
That anyone lives there, it is we who shall be homeless, outdoors

At the end. And we won't quite know what to do about it.
It's mind-boggling, actually. Each of us must try to concentrate
On some detail or other of their armor: somber, blood-red plumes
Floating over curved blue steel; the ribbed velvet stomacher
And its more social implications. Hurry to deal with the sting
Of added meaning, hurry to fend it off. Your lessons
Will become the ground of which we are made
And shall look back on, for awhile. Life was pleasant there.
And though we made it all up, it could still happen to us again.
Only then, watch out. The burden of proof of the implausible
Picaresque tale, boxes within boxes, will be yours
Next time round. And nobody is going to like your ending.

We had, though, a feeling of security
But we weren't aware of it then: that's
How secure we were. Now, in the dungeon of Better Living,
It seems we may be called back and interrogated about it
Which would be unfortunate, since only the absence of memory
Animates us as we walk briskly back and forth
At one with the soulless, restless crowd on the somber avenue.
Is there something new to see, to speculate on? Dunno, better
Stand back until something comes along to explain it,
This curious lack of anxiety that begins to gnaw
At one. Did it come because happiness hardened everything
In its fire, and so the forms cannot die, like a ruined
Fort too strong to be pulled down? And something like pale
Alpine flowers still flourishes there:
Some reminder that can never be anything more than that,
Yet its balm cares about something, we cannot be really naked
Having this explanation. So a reflected image of oneself
Manages to stay alive through the darkest times, a period
Of unprecedented frost, during which we get up each morning
And go about our business as usual.

And though there are some who leave regularly
For the patchwork landscape of childhood, north of here,
Our own kind of stiff standing around, waiting helplessly
And mechanically for instructions that never come, suits the space
Of our intense, uncommunicated speculation, marries
The still life of crushed, red fruit in the sky and tames it
For observation purposes. One is almost content
To be with people then, to read their names and summon
Greetings and speculation, or even nonsense syllables and
Diagrams from those who appear so brilliantly at ease
In the atmosphere we made by getting rid of most amenities
In the interests of a bare, strictly patterned life that apparently
Has charms we weren't even conscious of, which is
All to the good, except that it fumbles the premise
We put by, saving it for a later phase of intelligence, and now
We are living on it, ready to grow and make mistakes again,
Still standing on one leg while emerging continually
Into an inexpressive void, the blighted fields
Of a kiss, the rope of a random, unfortunate
Observation still around our necks though we thought we
Had cast it off in a novel that has somehow gotten stuck
To our lives, battening on us. A sad condition
To see us in, yet anybody
Will realize that he or she has made those same mistakes,
Memorized those same lists in the due course of the process
Being served on you now. Acres of bushes, treetops;
Orchards where the quince and apple seem to come and go
Mysteriously over long periods of time; waterfalls
And what they conceal, including what comes after—roads and roadways
Paved for the gently probing, transient automobile;
Farragoes of flowers; everything, in short,
That makes this explicit earth what it appears to be in our
Glassiest moments when a canoe shoots out from under some foliage
Into the river and finds it calm, not all that exciting but above all

Nothing to be afraid of, celebrates us
And what we have made of it.

Not something so very strange, but then seeming ordinary
Is strange too. Only the way we feel about the everything
And not the feeling itself is strange, strange to us, who live
And want to go on living under the same myopic stars we have known
Since childhood, when, looking out a window, we saw them
And immediately liked them.

And we can get back to that raw state
Of feeling, so long deemed
Inconsequential and therefore appropriate to our later musings
About religion, about migrations. What is restored
Becomes stronger than the loss as it is remembered;
Is a new, separate life of its own. A new color. Seriously blue.
Unquestioning. Acidly sweet. Must we then pick up the pieces
(But what are the pieces, if not separate puzzles themselves,
And meanwhile rain abrades the window?) and move to a central clearing-
    house
Somewhere in Iowa, far from the distant bells and thunderclaps that
Make this environment pliant and distinct? Nobody
Asked me to stay here, at least if they did I forgot, but I can
Hear the dust at the pores of the wood, and know then
The possibility of something more liberated and gracious
Though not of this time. Failing
That there are the books we haven't read, and just beyond them
A landscape stippled by frequent glacial interventions
That holds so well to its lunette one wants to keep it but we must
Go on despising it until that day when environment
Finally reads as a necessary but still vindictive opposition
To all caring, all explaining. Your finger traces a
Bleeding violet line down the columns of an old directory and to this
    spongy

State of talking things out a glass exclamation point opposes
A discrete claim: forewarned. So the voluminous past
Accepts, recycles our claims to present consideration
And the urban landscape is once again untroubled, smooth
As wax. As soon as the oddity is flushed out
It becomes monumental and anxious once again, looking
Down on our lives as from a baroque pinnacle and not the
Mosquito that was here twenty minutes ago.
The past absconds
With our fortunes just as we were rounding a major
Bend in the swollen river; not to see ahead
Becomes the only predicament when what
Might be sunken there is mentioned only
In crabbed allusions but will be back tomorrow.

It takes only a minute revision, and see—the thing
Is there in all its interested variegatedness,
With prospects and walks curling away, never to be followed,
A civilized concern, a never being alone.
Later on you'll have doubts about how it
Actually was, and certain greetings will remain totally forgotten,
As water forgets a dam once it's over it. But at this moment
A spirit of independence reigns. Quietude
To get out and do things in, and a rush back to the house
When evening turns up, and not a moment too soon.
Headhunters and jackals mingle with the viburnum
And hollyhocks outside, and it all adds up, pointedly,
To something one didn't quite admit feeling uneasy about, but now
That it's all out in the open, like a successful fire
Burning in a fireplace, really there's no cause for alarm.
For even when hours and days go by in silence and the phone
Never rings, and widely spaced drops of water
Fall from the eaves, nothing is any longer a secret
And one can live alone rejoicing in this:

That the years of war are far off in the past or the future,
That memory contains everything. And you see slipping down a hallway
The past self you decided not to have anything to do with any more
And it is a more comfortable you, dishonest perhaps,
But alive. Wanting you to know what you're losing.
And still the machinery of the great exegesis is only beginning
To groan and hum. There are moments like this one
That are almost silent, so that bird-watchers like us
Can come, and stay awhile, reflecting on shades of difference
In past performances, and move on refreshed.

But always and sometimes questioning the old modes
And the new wondering, the poem, growing up through the floor,
Standing tall in tubers, invading and smashing the ritual
Parlor, demands to be met on its own terms now,
Now that the preliminary negotiations are at last over.
You could be lying on the floor,
Or not have time for too much of any one thing,
Yet you know the song quickens in the bones
Of your neck, in your heel, and there is no point
In looking out over the yard where tractors run,
The empty space in the endless continuum
Of time has come up: the space that can be filled only by you.
And I had thought about the roadblocks, wondered
Why they were less frequent, wondered what progress the blizzard
Might have been making a certain distance back there,
But it was not enough to save me from choosing
Myself now, from being the place I have to get to
Before nightfall and under the shelter of trees
It is true but also without knowing out there in the dark,
Being alone at the center of a moan that did not issue from me
And is pulling me back toward old forms of address
I know I have already lived through, but they are strong again,
And big to fill the exotic spaces that arguing left.

So all the slightly more than young
Get moved up whether they like it or not, and only
The very old or the very young have any say in the matter,
Whether they are a train or a boat or just a road leading
Across a plain, from nowhere to nowhere. Later on
A record of the many voices of the middle-young will be issued
And found to be surprisingly original. That can't concern us,
However, because now there isn't space enough,
Not enough dimension to guarantee any kind of encounter
The stage-set it requires at the very least in order to burrow
Profitably through history and come out having something to say,
Even just one word with a slightly different intonation
To cause it to stand out from the backing of neatly invented
Chronicles of things men have said and done, like an English horn,
And then to sigh, to faint back
Into all our imaginings, dark
And viewless as they are,
Windows painted over with black paint but
We can sufficiently imagine, so much is admitted, what
Might be going on out there and even play some part
In the ordering of it all into lengths of final night,
Of dim play, of love that at lasts oozes through the seams
In the cement, suppurates, subsumes
All the other business of living and dying, the orderly
Ceremonials and handling of estates,
Checking what does not appear normal and drawing together
All the rest into the report that will finally be made
On a day when it does not appear that there is anything to receive it
Properly and we wonder whether we too are gone,
Buried in our love,
The love that defined us only for a little while,
And when it strolls back a few paces, to get another view,
Fears that it may have encountered eternity in the meantime.
And as the luckless describe love in glowing terms to strangers

In taverns, and the seemingly blessed may be unaware of having lost it,
So always there is a small remnant
Whose lives are congruent with their souls
And who ever afterward know no mystery in it,
The cimmerian moment in which all lives, all destinies
And incompleted destinies were swamped
As though by a giant wave that picks itself up
Out of a calm sea and retreats again into nowhere
Once its damage is done.
And what to say about those series
Of infrequent pellucid moments in which
One reads inscribed as though upon an empty page
The strangeness of all those contacts from the time they erupt
Soundlessly on the horizon and in a moment are upon you
Like a stranger on a snowmobile
But of which nothing can be known or written, only
That they passed this way? That to be bound over
To love in the dark, like Psyche, will somehow
Fill the sheaves of pages with a spidery, Spencerian hand
When all that will be necessary will be to go away
For a few minutes in order to return and find the work completed?
And so it is the only way
That love determines us, and we look the same
To others when they happen in afterwards, and cannot even know
We have changed, so massive in our difference
We are, like a new day that looks and cannot be the same
As those we used to reckon with, and so start
On our inane rounds again too dumb to profit from past
Mistakes—that's how different we are!

But once we have finished being interrupted
There is no longer any population to tell us how the gods
Had wanted it—only—so the story runs—a vast forest
With almost nobody in it. Your wants

Are still halfheartedly administered to; sometimes there is milk
And sometimes not, but a ladder of hilarious applause
No longer leads up to it. Instead, there's that cement barrier.
The forest ranger was nice, but warning us away,
Reminded you how other worlds can as easily take root
Like dandelions, in no time. There's no one here now
But émigrés, with abandoned skills, so near
To the surface of the water you can touch them through it.
It's they can tell you how love came and went
And how it keeps coming and going, ever disconcerting,
Even through the topiary trash of the present,
Its undoing, and smiles and seems to recognize no one.
It's all attitudinizing, maybe, images reflected off
Some mirrored surface we cannot see, and they seem both solid
As a suburban home and graceful phantasms, at ease
In any testing climate you may contrive. But surely
The slightly sunken memory that remains, accretes, is proof
That there were doings, yet no one admits to having heard
Even of these. You pass through lawns on the way to it; it's late
Even though the light is strongly yellow; and are heard
Commenting on how hard it is to get anybody to do anything
Any more; suddenly your name is remembered at the end—
It's there, on the list, was there all along
But now is too defunct to cope
Which may be better in the long run: we'll hear of
Other names, and know we don't want them, but that love
Was somehow given out to one of them by mistake,
Not utterly lost. Boyish, slipping past high school
Into the early forties, disingenuous though, yet all
The buds of this early spring won't open, which is surprising,
He says. It isn't likely to get any warmer than it is now.
In today's mainstream one mistakes him, sincerely, for someone else;
He passed on slowly and turns a corner. One can't say
He was gone before you knew it, yet something of that, some tepid

Challenge that was never taken up and disappeared forever,
Surrounds him. Love is after all for the privileged.

But there is something else—call it a consistent eventfulness,
A common appreciation of the way things have of enfolding
When your attention is distracted for a moment, and then
It's all bumps and history, as though this crusted surface
Had always been around, didn't just happen to come into being
A short time ago. The scarred afternoon is unfortunate
Perhaps, but as they come to see each other dimly
And for the first time, an internal romance
Of the situation rises in these human beings like sap
And they can at last know the fun of not having it all but
Having instead a keen appreciation of the ways in which it
Underachieves as well as rages: an appetite,
For want of a better word. In darkness and silence.

In the wind, it is living. What were the interruptions that
Led us here and then shanghaied us if not sincere attempts to
Understand and so desire another person, it doesn't
Matter which one, and then, self-abandoned, to build ourselves
So as to desire him fully, and at the last moment be
Taken aback at such luck: the feeling, invisible but alert.
On that clear February evening thirty-three years ago it seemed
A tapestry of living sounds shading to colors, and today
On this brick stump of an office building the colors are shaggy
Again, are at last what they once were, proving
They haven't changed: you have done that,
Not they. All that remains is to get to know them,
Like a twin brother from whom you were separated at birth
For whom the factory sounds now resonate in an uplifting
Sunset of your own choosing and fabrication, a rousing
Anthem to perpendicularity and the perennial exponential
Narration to cause everything to happen by evoking it

Within the framework of shared boredom and shared responsibilities.
Cheerful ads told us it was all going to be OK,
That the superstitions would do it all for you. But today
It's bigger and looser. People are not out to get you
And yet the walkways look dangerous. The smile slowly soured.
Still, coming home through all this
And realizing its vastness does add something to its dimension:
Teachers would never have stood for this. Which is why
Being tall and shy, you can still stand up more clearly
To the definition of what you are. You are not a sadist
But must only trust in the dismantling of that definition
Some day when names are being removed from things, when all attributes
Are sinking in the maelstrom of de-definition like spars.
You must then come up with something to say,
Anything, as long as it's no more than five minutes long,
And in the interval you shall have been washed. It's that easy.
But meanwhile, I know, stone tenements are still hoarding
The shadow that is mine; there is nothing to admit to,
No one to confess to. This period goes on for quite a few years
But as though along a low fence by a sidewalk. Then brandishes
New definitions in its fists, but these are evidently false
And get thrown out of court. Next you're on your own
In an old film about two guys walking across the United States.
The love that comes after will be richly satisfying,
Like rain on the desert, calling unimaginable diplomacy into being
Until you thought you should get off here, maybe this stop
Was yours. And then it all happens blindingly, over and over
In a continuous, vivid present that wasn't there before.
No need to make up stories at this juncture, everybody
Likes a joke and they find yours funny. And then it's just
Two giant steps down to the big needing and feeling
That is yours to grow in. Not grow old, the
Magic present still insists on being itself,
But to play in. To live and be lived by

And in this way bring all things to the sensible conclusion
Dreamed into their beginnings, and so arrive at the end.

Simultaneously in an area the size of West Virginia
The opposing view is climbing toward heaven: how swiftly
It rises! How slender the packed silver mass spiraling
Into further thinness, into what can only be called excess,
It seems, now. And anyway it sounds better in translation
Which is the only language you will read it in:
"I was lost, but seemed to be coming home,
Through quincunxes of apple trees, but ever
As I drew closer, as in Zeno's paradox, the mirage
Of home withdrew and regrouped a little farther off.
I could see white curtains fluttering at the windows
And in the garden under a big brass-tinted apple tree
The old man had removed his hat and was gazing at the grass
As though in sorrow, sorrow for what I had done.
Realizing it was now or never, I lurched
With one supreme last effort out of the dream
Onto the couch-grass behind the little red-painted palings:
I was here! But it all seemed so lonesome. I was welcomed
Without enthusiasm. My room had been kept as it was
But the windows were closed, there was a smell of a closed room.
And though I have been free ever since
To browse at will through my appetites, lingering
Over one that seemed special, the lamplight
Can never replace the sad light of early morning
Of the day I left, convinced (as indeed I am today)
Of the logic of my search, yet all unprepared
To look into the practical aspects, the whys and wherefores,
And so never know, eventually, whether I have accomplished
My end, or merely returned, another leaf that falls."
One must be firm not to be taken in by the histrionics
And even more by the rigorous logic with which the enemy

Deploys his message like iron trenches under ground
That rise here and there in blunt, undulating shapes.
And once you have told someone that none of it frightens you
There is still the breached sense of your own being
To live with, to somehow nurse back to plenitude:
Yet it never again has that hidden abundance,
That relaxed, joyous well-being with which
In other times it frolicked along roads, making
The best of ignorance and unconscious, innocent selfishness,
The spirit that was to occupy those times
Now transposed, sunk too deep in its own reflection
For memory. The eager calm of every day.
But in the end the dark stuff, the odd quick attack
Followed by periods of silence that get shorter and shorter
Resolves the subjective-versus-objective approach by undoing
The complications of our planet, its climate, its sonatinas
And stories, its patches of hard ugly snow waiting around
For spring to melt them. And it keeps some memories of the troubled
Beginning-to-be-resolved period even in the timely first inkling
Of maturity in March, "when night and day grow equal," but even
More in the solemn peach-harvest that happens some months later
After differing periods of goofing-off and explosive laughter.
To be always articulating these preludes, there seems to be no
Sense in it, if it is going to be perpetually five o'clock
With the colors of the bricks seeping more and more bloodlike through the
   tan
Of trees, and then only to blacken. But it says more
About us. When they finally come
With much laborious jangling of keys to unlock your cell
You can tell them yourself what it is,
Who you are, and how you happened to turn out this way,
And how they made you, for better or for worse, what you are now,
And how you seem to be, neither humble nor proud, *frei aber einsam.*

And should anyone question the viability of this process
You can point to the accessible result. Not like a great victory
That tirelessly sweeps over mankind again and again at the end
Of each era, presuming you can locate it, for the greater good
Of history, though you are not the first person to confuse
Its solicitation with something like scorn, but the slow polishing
Of an infinitely tiny cage big enough to hold all the dispiritedness,
Contempt, and incorrect conclusions based on false premises that now
Slow you down but by that time, enchaliced, will sound attentive,
Tonic even, an antidote to badly reasoned desiring: footfalls
Of the police approaching gingerly through the soft spring air.

At Pine Creek imitation the sky was no nearer. The difference
Was microtones, a seasoning between living and gestures.
It emerged as a rather stiff impression
Of all things. Not that there aren't those glad to have
A useful record like this to add to the collection
In the portfolio. But beyond just needing where is the need
To carry heaven around in one's breast-pocket? To satisfy
The hunger of millions with something more substantial than good wishes
And still withhold the final reassurance? So you see these
Days each with its disarming set of images and attitudes
Are beneficial perhaps but only after the last one
In every series has disappeared, down the road, forever, at night.

It would be cockier to ask of heaven just what is this present
Of an old dishpan you bestowed on me? Can I get out the door
With it, now that so many old enmities and flirtations have shrunk
To little more than fine print in the contexts of lives and so much
New ground is coming undone, shaken out like a scarf or a handkerchief
From this window that dominates everything perhaps a little too much?
In falling we should note the protective rush of air past us
And then pray for some day after the war to cull each of

The limited set of reflections we were given at the beginning
To try to make a fortune out of. Only then will some kind of radical stance
Have had some meaning, and for itself, not for us who lie gasping
On slopes never having had the nerve to trust just us, to go out with us,
Not fearing some solemn overseer in the breath from the treetops.

And that that game-plan and the love we have been given for nothing
In particular should coincide—no, it is not yet time to think these things.
In vain would one try to peel off that love from the object it fits
So nicely, now, remembering it will have to be some day. You
Might as well offer it to your neighbor, the first one you meet, or throw
It away entirely, as plan to unlock on such and such a date
The door to this forest that has been your total upbringing.
No one expects it, and thus
Flares are launched out over the late disturbed landscape
Of items written down only to be forgotten once more, forever this time.

And already the sky is getting to be less salmon-colored,
The black clouds more meaningless (otter-shaped at first;
Now, as they retreat into incertitude, mere fins)
And perhaps it's too late for anything like the overhaul
That seemed called for, earlier, but whose initiative
Was it after all? I mean I don't mind staying here
A little longer, sitting quietly under a tree, if all this
Is going to clear up by itself anyway.

There is no indication this will happen,
But I don't mind. I feel at peace with the parts of myself
That questioned this other, easygoing side, chafed it
To a knotted rope of guesswork looming out of storms
And darkness and proceeding on its way into nowhere
Barely muttering. Always, a few errands
Summon us periodically from the room of our forethought
And that is a good thing. And such attentiveness

Besides! Almost more than anybody could bring to anything,
But we managed it, and with a good grace, too. Nobody
Is going to hold *that* against us. But since you bring up the question
I will say I am not unhappy to place myself entirely
At your disposal temporarily. Much that had drained out of living
Returns, in those moments, mounting the little capillaries
Of polite questions and seeming concern. I want it back.

And though that other question that I asked and can't
Remember any more is going to move still farther upward, casting
Its shadow enormously over where I remain, I can't see it.
Enough to know that I shall have answered for myself soon,
Be led away for further questioning and later returned
To the amazingly quiet room in which all my life has been spent.
It comes and goes; the walls, like veils, are never the same,
Yet the thirst remains identical, always to be entertained
And marveled at. And it is finally we who break it off,
Speed the departing guest, lest any question remain
Unasked, and thereby unanswered. Please, it almost
Seems to say, take me with you, I'm old enough. Exactly.
And so each of us has to remain alone, conscious of each other
Until the day when war absolves us of our differences. We'll
Stay in touch. So they have it, all the time. But all was strange.

INDEX

The poems in this collection originally appeared in *The American Poetry Review, Antaeus, Apparitions, Art and Literature, Best in Company, Big Table, Broadway, Cicada, Cincinnati Poetry Review, The Columbia Forum, Contemporary Poets Calendar* (1980), *The Denver Quarterly, Folder, The Georgia Review, Grand Street, Harper's Magazine, Harvard Advocate, Harvard Magazine, The Iowa Review, Kenyon Review, Locations, Locus Solus, New American Review, The New York Review of Books, The New Yorker, The Ohio Review, The Paris Review, Partisan Review, Ploughshares, Poetry, Quarterly Review of Literature, Roof, Spectator, Sulphur, Sun, Times Literary Supplement, Vanderbilt Poetry Review, The Virginia Quarterly Review, Vogue, The Yale Review, Z, Zero,* and in the author's earlier books *Some Trees, Rivers and Mountains, The Double Dream of Spring,* published by The Ecco Press, and in *Three Poems, Self-Portrait in a Convex Mirror, Houseboat Days, As You Know, Shadow Trains,* and *A Wave,* published by Viking Penguin Inc.

PENGUIN POETS